Kaplan Publishing are constantly finding new ways to support students looking for exam success and our online resources really do add an extra dimension to your studies.

This book comes with free MyKaplan online resources so that you can study anytime, anywhere. **This free online resource is not sold separately and is included in the price of the book.**

Having purchased this book, you have access to the following online study materials:

CONTENT	AAT	
	Text	Kit
Electronic version of the book	✓	✓
Knowledge Check tests with instant answers	✓	
Mock assessments online	✓	✓
Material updates	✓	✓

D1368268

How to access your online resources

Kaplan Financial students will already have a MyKaplan account and these extra resources will be available to you online. You do not need to register again, as this process was completed when you enrolled. If you are having problems accessing online materials, please ask your course administrator.

If you are not studying with Kaplan and did not purchase your book via a Kaplan website, to unlock your extra online resources please go to www.mykaplan.co.uk/add-online-resources (even if you have set up an account and registered books previously). You will then need to enter the ISBN number (on the title page and back cover) and the unique pass key number contained in the scratch panel below to gain access. You will also be required to enter additional information during this process to set up or confirm your account details.

If you purchased through the Kaplan Publishing website you will automatically receive an e-mail invitation to MyKaplan. Please register your details using this email to gain access to your content. If you do not receive the e-mail or book content, please contact Kaplan Publishing.

Your Code and Information

This code can only be used once for the registration of one book online. This registration and your online content will expire when the final sittings for the examinations covered by this book have taken place. Please allow one hour from the time you submit your book details for us to process your request.

Please scratch the film to access your unique code.

Please be aware that this code is case-sensitive and you will need to include the dashes within the passcode, but not when entering the ISBN.

KAPLAN

PUBLISHING

AAT

Q2022

Business Tax
(Finance Act 2021)

EXAM KIT

This Exam Kit supports study for the following AAT qualifications:

AAT Professional Diploma in Accounting – Level 4

AAT Level 4 Diploma in Business Skills

AAT Professional Diploma in Accounting at SCQF Level 8

PUBLISHING

British Library Cataloguing-in-Publication Data

A catalogue record for this book is available from the British Library.

Published by:

Kaplan Publishing UK

Unit 2 The Business Centre

Molly Millar's Lane

Wokingham

Berkshire

RG41 2QZ

ISBN: 978-1-83996-066-6

Acknowledgements

We are grateful to HM Revenue and Customs for the provision of tax forms, which are Crown Copyright and are reproduced here with kind permission from the Office of Public Sector Information.

CONTENTS

Features in this exam kit

In addition to providing a wide ranging bank of real assessment style questions, we have also included in this kit:

- unit specific information and advice on assessment technique
- our recommended approach to make your revision for this particular unit as effective as possible.

You will find a wealth of other resources to help you with your studies on the Kaplan and AAT websites:

www.mykaplan.co.uk

www.aat.org.uk/

Quality and accuracy are of the utmost importance to us so if you spot an error in any of our products, please send an email to mykaplanreporting@kaplan.com with full details, or follow the link to the feedback form in MyKaplan.

Our Quality Coordinator will work with our technical team to verify the error and take action to ensure it is corrected in future editions.

UNIT SPECIFIC INFORMATION

THE EXAM

FORMAT OF THE ASSESSMENT

The assessment for this unit consists of 11 compulsory, independent, tasks.

Students will be assessed by computer-based assessment.

In any one assessment, students may not be assessed on all content, or on the full depth or breadth of a piece of content. The content assessed may change over time to ensure validity of assessment, but all assessment criteria will be tested over time.

The learning outcomes for this unit are as follows:

	Learning outcome	Weighting
1	Prepare tax computations for sole traders and partnerships	25%
2	Prepare tax computations for limited companies	15%
3	Prepare tax computations for the sale of capital assets by limited companies	15%
4	Understand administrative requirements of the UK's tax regime	15%
5	Understand the tax implications of business disposals	10%
6	Understand tax reliefs, tax planning opportunities and agent's responsibilities in reporting taxation to HM Revenue & Customs	20%
	Total	100%

Time allowed

2 hours

PASS MARK

The pass mark for all AAT CBAs is 70%.

 Always keep your eye on the clock and make sure you attempt all questions!

DETAILED SYLLABUS

The detailed syllabus and study guide written by the AAT can be found at:

www.aat.org.uk/

INDEX TO QUESTIONS AND ANSWERS

KAPLAN PUBLISHING

		Page number	
		Question	Answer
Business disposals			
72	Susan and Rachel	83	185
73	Norman	84	186
74	Harry and Briony	86	188
75	Cheryl	87	189
76	Ralf	88	191
77	Stephan	89	193
78	Leigh	91	195

EXAM TECHNIQUE

- **Do not skip any of the material** in the syllabus.

- **Read each question** very carefully.

- **Double-check your answer** before committing yourself to it.

- Answer **every** question – if you do not know an answer to a multiple choice question or true/false question, you don't lose anything by guessing. Think carefully before you **guess**.

- If you are answering a multiple-choice question, **eliminate first those answers that you know are wrong**. Then choose the most appropriate answer from those that are left.

- **Don't panic** if you realise you've answered a question incorrectly. Getting one question wrong will not mean the difference between passing and failing.

Computer-based assessments – tips

- Do not attempt a CBA until you have **completed all study material** relating to it.

- On the AAT website there is a CBA demonstration. It is **ESSENTIAL** that you attempt this before your real CBA. You will become familiar with how to move around the CBA screens and the way that questions are formatted, increasing your confidence and speed in the actual assessment.

- Be sure you understand how to use the **software** before you start the assessment. If in doubt, ask the assessment centre staff to explain it to you.

- Questions are **displayed on the screen** and answers are entered using keyboard and mouse. At the end of the assessment, you are given a certificate showing the result you have achieved unless some manual marking is required for the assessment.

- In addition to the traditional multiple-choice question type, CBAs will also contain **other types of questions**, such as number entry questions, drag and drop, true/false, pick lists or drop down menus or hybrids of these.

- In some CBAs you may have to type in complete computations or written answers.

- You need to be sure you **know how to answer questions** of this type before you sit the real assessment, through practice.

KAPLAN'S RECOMMENDED REVISION APPROACH

QUESTION PRACTICE IS THE KEY TO SUCCESS

Success in professional examinations relies upon you acquiring a firm grasp of the required knowledge at the tuition phase. In order to be able to do the questions, knowledge is essential.

However, the difference between success and failure often hinges on your assessment technique on the day and making the most of the revision phase of your studies.

The **Kaplan study text** is the starting point, designed to provide the underpinning knowledge to tackle all questions. However, in the revision phase, poring over text books is not the answer.

Kaplan pocket notes are designed to help you quickly revise a topic area; however you then need to practise questions. There is a need to progress to assessment style questions as soon as possible, and to tie your assessment technique and technical knowledge together.

The importance of question practice cannot be over-emphasised.

The recommended approach below is designed by expert tutors in the field, in conjunction with their knowledge of the chief assessor and the sample assessment.

You need to practise as many questions as possible in the time you have left.

OUR AIM

Our aim is to get you to the stage where you can attempt assessment questions confidently, to time, in a closed book environment, with no supplementary help (i.e. to simulate the real assessment experience).

Practising your assessment technique is also vitally important for you to assess your progress and identify areas of weakness that may need more attention in the final run up to the real assessment.

In order to achieve this we recognise that initially you may feel the need to practise some questions with open book help.

Good assessment technique is vital.

THE KAPLAN REVISION PLAN

Stage 1: Assess areas of strength and weakness

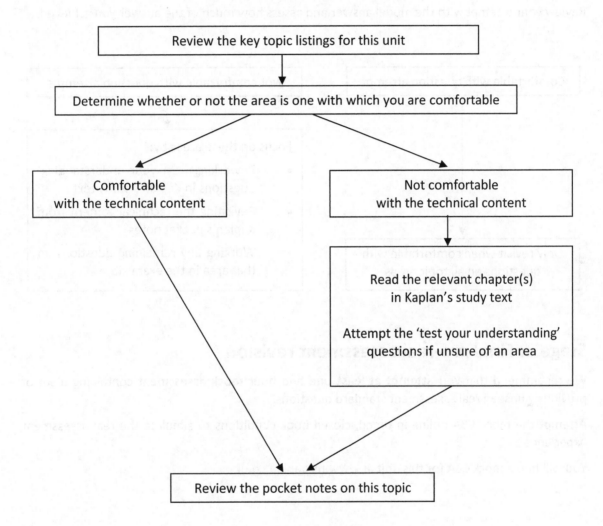

Stage 2: Practise questions

Follow the order of revision of topics as presented in this kit and attempt the questions in the order suggested.

Try to avoid referring to study texts and your notes and the model answer until you have completed your attempt.

Review your attempt with the model answer and assess how much of the answer you achieved.

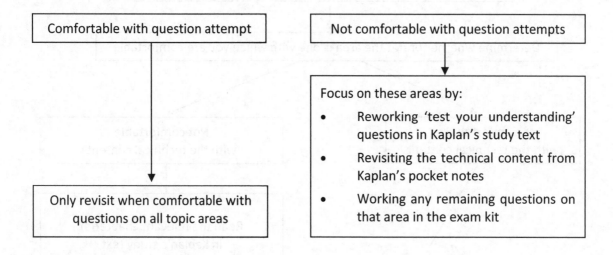

Comfortable with question attempt	Not comfortable with question attempts

Focus on these areas by:

- Reworking 'test your understanding' questions in Kaplan's study text
- Revisiting the technical content from Kaplan's pocket notes
- Working any remaining questions on that area in the exam kit

Only revisit when comfortable with questions on all topic areas

Stage 3: Final pre-real assessment revision

We recommend that you **attempt at least one two hour mock assessment** containing a set of previously unseen real assessment standard questions.

Attempt the mock CBA online in timed, closed book conditions to simulate the real assessment experience.

You will find a mock CBA for this unit at www.mykaplan.co.uk

REFERENCE MATERIAL

Reference material is provided in this assessment. During your assessment you will be able to access reference material through a series of clickable links on the right of every task. These will produce pop-up windows which can be moved or closed.

The reference material has been included in this Exam Kit (below). This is based on the version of the reference material that was available at the time of going to print.

The full version of the reference material is available for download from the AAT website.

Level 4 Business Tax (BNTA)
reference material

Finance Act 2021 – for Q2022 assessments in 2022 and 2023

Reference material for AAT assessment of Business Tax

Introduction

This document comprises data that you may need to consult during your Business Tax computer-based assessment.

The material can be consulted during the practice and live assessments by using the reference materials section at each task position. It's made available here so you can familiarise yourself with the content before the assessment.

Do not take a print of this document into the exam room with you*.

This document may be changed to reflect periodical updates in the computer-based assessment, so please check you have the most recent version while studying. This version is based on **Finance Act 2021** and is for use in AAT Q2022 assessments in 2022 and 2023.

*Unless you need a printed version as part of reasonable adjustments for particular needs, in which case you must discuss this with your tutor at least six weeks before the assessment date.

Contents

1. Income tax

Trading allowance			£1,000
Personal allowance			£12,570
	Basic rate (0-£37,700)	Higher rate (£37,701 - £150,000)	Additional rate (Above £150,000)
Salary	20%	40%	45%
Dividends	7.5%	32.5%	38.1%
Trading income	20%	40%	45%

- Income tax computations will not be required in the assessment, but the rates may be used in tax planning discussions.

2. Income tax basis period rules

Ongoing business	Current year basis		
Year of commencement	Actual basis		
Second tax year	Accounting period <12 months ends in the year	Accounting period ≥12 months ends in the year	No accounting period ends in year
	Tax first 12 months of trade	Tax 12 months to accounting date	Actual basis
Third tax year	Tax 12 months to the accounting date		
Final tax year	Tax from end of basis period in previous tax year to the date of cessation. Deduct overlap profits		

3. National Insurance (NI)

Class 2 contributions	£3.05 per week
Small profits threshold	£6,515
Class 4 contributions on trading profits between £9,568 and £50,270	9%
Class 4 contributions on trading profits above £50,270	2%

- Dividends are not subject to NI
- Salaries are subject to:
  - employee NI at 12% between £9,568 and £50,270 and 2% above £50,270
  - employer NI at 13.8% above £8,840 (an employment allowance of £4,000 is available)
- Calculations of NI on salaries will not be required in the assessment but the rates may be used in tax planning discussions.

4. Capital gains tax

Annual exempt amount	£12,300
Basic rate	10%
Higher rate	20%
Business asset disposal relief rate	10%
Business asset disposal relief lifetime allowance	£1,000,000

5. Corporation tax

Rate of corporation tax	19%

6. Capital allowances

Annual investment allowance	£1,000,000
Writing down allowance – assets other than motor cars	18%
Super deduction – expenditure by companies after 1 April 2021	130%
Writing down allowance cars:	
- CO2 emissions 0g/km	100%
- CO2 emissions up to 50 g/km	18%
- CO2 emissions over 50 g/km	6%
Small pools allowance	£1,000
Structures and buildings allowance	3%

7. Disallowed expenditure

Type of expense	Disallowable in calculation of trading profit	Notes
Fines and penalties	Fines on the business Fines on directors/owners	Employee fines are not disallowed if incurred in the course of their employment.
Donations	Political donations Donations to national charities	Donations to local charities are allowable (these will only be examined for unincorporated businesses).
Capital expenditure	Depreciation Loss on disposal Capital items expensed	Capital allowances may be available.
Legal and professional	Relating to: - capital items - purchase/renewal of a long lease - purchase of a short lease (50 years or less) - breaches of law/regulations.	Legal fees on the renewal of a short lease (50 years or less) are allowable.
Entertaining and gifts	Customer gifts (unless <£50 per annum, not food, drink, tobacco, or cash vouchers and contains business advertising). Customer/supplier entertaining.	Staff gifts and staff entertaining are allowable.
Cars	Depreciation. Private use by owners. 15% of lease cost if leased car >50g/km CO_2 emissions.	
Private expenditure of owner (unincorporated businesses only)	Goods taken for own use. Salary of owners. Private use % by owners. Private expenditure, e.g., class 2 and 4 NICs, legal and professional fees for personal expenditure.	Reasonable salaries of family members are allowable.

8. Trading losses

Loss option	Sole trader/Partner	Company
Carry forward	Against future profits of the same trade only. Applies automatically to first available profits. Applies after any other elections or if no elections are made.	Losses not relieved in the current accounting period or previous 12 months are carried forward and an election can be made to set against total profits in future periods.
Current year/carry back	Against total income in the current and/or previous tax year in any order. If opted for in either year, the amount of loss used cannot be restricted to preserve the personal allowance. Make claim by 31 January 2024 for 2021/22 tax year.	Can elect to set trading losses against current accounting period 'total profits'. Qualifying charitable donations will remain unrelieved. If the above election is made, can also carry back trading loss to set against 'total profits' within the previous 12 months. Claim within 2 years of the end of the loss-making period.
Opening year loss relief – loss in first four years of trade	Against total income of the previous three tax years on a FIFO basis. If opted for, losses will be used to reduce total income as much as possible in each year and cannot be restricted to preserve the personal allowance. Make claim by 31 January 2024 for 2021/22 tax year.	N/A
Terminal loss relief	Against trading profits of the previous 3 years on a LIFO basis. Claim within 4 years from the end of the last tax year of trade.	Against total profits of the previous 3 years. Claim within 2 years of the end of the loss-making period.

9. Chargeable gains – Reliefs

Relief	Conditions
Replacement of business assets (Rollover) relief	Available to individuals and companies. Examinable for companies. Qualifying assets (original and replacement) – must be used in a trade and be land and buildings or fixed plant and machinery. Qualifying time period – replacement asset must be purchased between one year before and three years after the sale of the original asset. Partial reinvestment – if only some of the sales proceeds reinvested then the gain taxable is the lower of the full gain and the proceeds not reinvested.
Gift relief (holdover relief)	Available to individuals only. Qualifying assets – assets used in the trade of the donor or the donor's personal company, shares in any unquoted trading company or shares in the donors personal trading company. A personal trading company is one where the donor has at least 5%.
Business asset disposal relief	Available to individuals only. Gain taxable at 10%. £1m lifetime limit For 2021/22 a claim must be made by 31 January 2024. Qualifying assets: - the whole or part of a business carried on by the individual (alone or in partnership). The assets must have been owned for 24 months prior to sale - assets of the individual's or partnership's trading business that has now ceased. The assets must have been owned for 24 months prior to cessation and sale must be within 3 years of cessation - shares in the individual's 'personal trading company' (own at least 5%). The individual must have owned the shares and been an employee of the company for 24 months prior to sale.

10. Payment and administration

	Sole traders/partners	Company
Filing date	31 October following the end of the tax year if filing a paper return. 31 January following the end of the tax year if filing online. Amendments can be made within 12 months of filing.	Filed on the later of 12 months after end of AP or 3 months after the notice to deliver a tax return has been issued. Company can amend return within 12 months of the filing date.
Payment date	31 January following the end of the tax year. If payments on accounts are due: • first POA – 31 January during tax year • second POA – 31 July after tax year • balancing payment – 31 January after tax year. POA's are each 50% of the previous years income tax and class 4 NICS due by self-assessment. POA's are not required for capital gains or class 2 NICs. POA's are not due if prior year tax payable by self-assessment is less than £1,000 OR if >80% of prior year tax was collected at source.	Small companies (annual profits less than £1.5 million): 9 months + 1 day after end of the accounting period (AP). Large companies (annual profits greater than £1.5 million) must estimate the year's tax liability and pay 25% of the estimate on the 14th day of each of the 7th, 10th, 13th and 16th month from the start of the accounting period.
Interest	Charged daily on late payment	Interest charged daily on late payment. Overpayment of tax receives interest from HMRC. Interest is taxable/tax allowable as interest income.
Penalties for late filing	£100. After 3 months, £10 per day for up to 90 days. After 6 months, 5% tax due (or £300 if greater). After 12 months, 5% tax due (or £300 if greater) if not deliberate. After 12 months, 70% of tax due (or £300 if greater) if deliberate and not concealed. After 12 months, 100% tax due (or £300 if greater) if deliberate and concealed.	£100. After 3 months, £100. After 6 months, 10% of unpaid tax. After 12 months, 10% of unpaid tax.
Late payment	30 days late – 5% of tax outstanding at that date. 6 months days late – 5% of tax outstanding at that date. 12 months late – 5% of tax outstanding at that date.	N/A
Notify of chargeability	5 October following the end of the tax year.	Within 3 months of starting to trade.

	Sole traders/partners	Company
Enquiry	Within 12 months of submission of return. Penalty for failure to produce enquiry documents = £300 + £60 per day.	Within 12 months of submission of return. Penalty for failure to produce enquiry documents: £300 + £60 per day.
Record retention	Five years from filing date. Penalty for failure to keep records is up to £3,000.	Six years after the end of the relevant accounting period. Penalty for failure to keep proper records is up to £3,000.

11. Penalties for incorrect returns

Type of behaviour	Maximum	Unprompted (minimum)	Prompted (minimum
Careless error and inaccuracy are due to failure to take reasonable care	30%	0%	15%
Deliberate error but not concealed	70%	20%	35%
Deliberate error and concealed	100%	30%	50%

The Association of Accounting Technicians
140 Aldersgate Street
London
EC1A 4HY
t: +44 (0)20 7397 3000
f: +44 (0)20 7397 3009
e: aat@aat.org.uk
aat.org.uk

Section 1

PRACTICE QUESTIONS

ADJUSTING ACCOUNTING PROFITS AND LOSSES FOR TAX PURPOSES

Key answer tips

Adjustment of profits and determining capital versus revenue expenditure are important areas and will be tested in Task 1 of the assessment.

Knowledge of what is treated as capital and what is not is often an area where learners slip up. It is important not to neglect learning facts such as these.

Adjustment of profits questions may include a computation starting from the accounting profit where you will need to adjust for disallowed expenses. It is important to carefully read the question and consider each item to decide whether it is allowable or not.

The Business Tax reference material provided in your assessment covers these topics in the section headed 'Disallowed expenditure'.

1   GILES

Giles is a sole trader and incurred the following expenditure.

(a)   **For each item of expenditure, tick the appropriate box to show whether the item is treated as revenue or capital expenditure.**

	Revenue	Capital
Decorating an office		
Computer for a salesman		
Office building extension		
Electricity for the quarter to 31 March 2022		
Meal to entertain a customer from Germany		
Fork lift truck for the warehouse		

Crush Ltd incurred the following expenditure.

(b)   For each item of expenditure, tick the appropriate box(es) to show whether the item will be treated as allowable or disallowable in the company's adjustment of trading profits computation, and whether or not capital allowances (CAs) will be available.

	Allowable	Disallowable	CAs available
Water rates			
Building insurance			
Replacement of factory machinery			
Replacement of a severely damaged roof on an office building			
Insurance for motor cars			
Parking fine incurred by an employee			

2   PHILIP

Philip is a sole trader and incurred the following expenditure.

(a)   For each item of expenditure, tick the appropriate box to show whether the item is treated as revenue or capital expenditure.

	Revenue	Capital
Printer for the office computer		
Water rates		
Legal fees for purchase of a building		

Flush Ltd incurred the following expenditure.

(b)   For each item of expenditure, tick the appropriate box(es) to show whether the item will be treated as allowable or disallowable in the company's adjustment of trading profits computation, and whether or not plant and machinery capital allowances (CAs) will be available.

	Allowable	Disallowable	CAs available
Painting an office			
Car for a salesman			
Office building extension			
Gas for the quarter to 30 June 2022			
Van for deliveries			
Meal to entertain staff			
Printer for the office computer			
Dividends payable			
Costs of a fraud carried out by a director. These costs are not covered by insurance.			

3   BROWN

Brown is a sole trader and incurred the following expenditure.

(a)   **For each item of expenditure, tick the appropriate box to show whether the item is treated as revenue or capital expenditure.**

	Revenue	Capital
Repairs to a boiler		
Insurance for motor cars		
Replacement of a severely damaged roof on a newly-purchased warehouse before being able to use the building		
Parking fine incurred by Brown		

Armadillo is self-employed and his business has made a profit of £34,890 in the year ended 31 March 2022.

This is after the inclusion of the following expenditure:

- Depreciation of £2,345.

- Motor expenses of £4,788. This relates equally to two cars both of which are used 50% for private journeys, one by Armadillo and one by an employee.

- Staff Christmas party of £2,570, which worked out at £257 per head.

- Gift aid donation of £34.

- Wages to Armadillo's wife of £19,000. Other members of staff with the same job in the business are paid £14,500.

- Capital allowances have been calculated at £3,460.

(b)   **Calculate Armadillo's tax adjusted trading profits for the year ended 31 March 2022 using the following pro forma.**

Where an item does not require adjustment insert a 0. Where an item is to be deducted from accounting profit, this should be shown as a negative figure, either using a minus sign or brackets.

	£
Accounting profit	34,890
Depreciation	
Motor expenses	
Staff Christmas party	
Gift aid donation	
Wages to Armadillo's wife	
Capital allowances	
Taxable profit	

4   FINN

Finn is self-employed and has a business making widgets.

The business has the following statement of profit or loss for the year ended 31 March 2022:

	£	£
Turnover		1,360,250
Less: Cost of sales		(776,780)
Gross profit		583,470
Wages and salaries	147,280	
Rent and rates	65,280	
Repairs	30,760	
Advertising and entertaining	27,630	
Accountancy and legal costs	16,260	
Motor expenses	38,000	
Leasing costs	8,000	
Telephone and office costs	15,200	
Depreciation	26,525	
Other expenses	101,265	
		(476,200)
Net profit		107,270

Additional information:

1   Repairs include:

	£
Redecorating Finn's flat	10,000
Decorating business premises	12,000

2   Advertising and entertaining includes:

	£
Gifts to customers:	
Food hampers costing £25 each	1,050
Pens carrying the business's logo, costing £5 each	400
Sponsorship of local charity fete	5,300

3   Motor expenses comprise the running costs of:

	£
Delivery vans	22,000
Sales representative's car	10,000
Finn's car which is 50% used for private mileage	6,000

4   Leasing costs of £8,000 are for the sales representative's car which has CO_2 emissions of 85g/km.

5   Other expenses include:

	£
Donation to Children in Need (a national charity)	500
Health and safety fine	400

6   Capital allowances have already been calculated at £21,070.

Calculate Finn's tax adjusted trading profits for the year ended 31 March 2022 using the following pro forma.

Where an item does not require adjustment insert a 0. Where an item is to be deducted from accounting profit, this should be shown as a negative figure, either using a minus sign or brackets.

	£
Accounting profit	107,270
Wages and salaries	
Rent and rates	
Repairs	
Advertising and entertaining	
Accountancy and legal costs	
Motor expenses	
Leasing costs	
Telephone and office costs	
Depreciation	
Other expenses	
Capital allowances	
Taxable profit	

5 **JAMIE**

Jamie's food manufacturing business has the following statement of profit or loss for the year ended 31 March 2022:

	£	£
Turnover		835,280
Less: Cost of sales		(437,528)
Gross profit		397,752
Wages and salaries	165,948	
Rent, rates and insurance	50,100	
Motor expenses	26,250	
Depreciation	40,355	
Other expenses	137,165	
		(419,818)
Net loss		(22,066)

Additional information:

1   Wages and salaries include:

	£
Jamie	28,000
Jamie's wife Sue, who does not work in the business	12,500
Jamie's daughter, Lisa, the Financial Controller of the business	21,425

2   Motor expenses comprise the running costs of:

	£
Delivery vans	17,940
Salesman's car	6,060
Jamie's motorbike (30% private use)	2,250

3   Other expenses include:

	£
Entertaining customers	625
Entertaining staff (Christmas party)	300
Cost of recipe books given to customers, each with the business logo clearly showing, costing £12.50 each	750
Cost of staff training	1,015

4   Jamie had taken two tins of caviar to eat at home. He paid the business the cost price of £50 each for these tins. Their selling price was £200 each.

5   Capital allowances have already been calculated at £42,236.

Calculate Jamie's tax adjusted trading profits for the year ended 31 March 2022 using the following pro forma.

Where an item does not require adjustment insert a 0. Where an item is to be deducted from accounting loss, this should be shown as a negative figure, either using a minus sign or brackets.

	£
Accounting loss	(22,066)
Jamie's salary	
Sue's salary	
Lisa's salary	
Rents, rates and insurance	
Delivery van expenses	
Salesman's car expenses	
Jamie's motorbike expenses	
Depreciation	
Entertaining customers	
Entertaining staff	
Recipe books	
Cost of staff training	
Caviar	
Capital allowances	
Taxable profit/(loss)	

6   REBECCA

Rebecca runs a beauty salon and lives in the small flat above the salon.

Her business has the following statement of profit or loss for the year ended 31 March 2022:

	£	£
Turnover		351,822
Less: Cost of sales		(208,178)
Gross profit		143,644
Profit on sale of equipment		1,280
		144,924
Professional fees	980	
Impaired debts	1,540	
Repairs and maintenance	340	
Depreciation	7,424	
Heating	2,240	
Rent, rates and insurance	12,000	
Motor expenses	7,780	
Wages and salaries	30,936	
Telephone and office costs	742	
Miscellaneous expenses	1,778	
		(65,760)
Net profit		79,164

Additional information:

1   Professional fees comprise:

	£
Accountancy fees	720
Payroll fees	260

2   Impaired debts comprise:

	£
Increase in specific impaired debt provision	800
Increase in general impaired debt provision	268
Trade debts written off	672
Trade debts recovered	(200)

3   Rent, rates and insurance include expenses relating to the flat where Rebecca lives of £3,000.

4   Motor expenses comprise the running costs of:

	£
Van expenses (van used by Rebecca exclusively for the business)	5,090
Car expenses (car used by Rebecca exclusively for private purposes)	2,690

5   Wages and salaries include Rebecca's drawings of £18,000.

6   Miscellaneous expenses include:

	£
Gifts of diaries to customers costing £7 each and bearing the logo of the business	798
Parking fines incurred by Rebecca in the van	280

7   One of your colleagues has calculated Rebecca's capital allowances to be £11,642.

Calculate Rebecca's tax adjusted trading profits for the year ended 31 March 2022 using the following pro forma.

Where an item does not require adjustment insert a 0. Where an item is to be deducted from accounting profit, this should be shown as a negative figure, either using a minus sign or brackets.

	£
Accounting profit	79,164
Profit on sale of equipment	
Accountancy fees	
Payroll fees	
Increase in specific impaired debt provision	
Increase in general impaired debt provision	
Trade debts written off	
Trade debts recovered	
Repairs and maintenance	
Depreciation	
Heating	
Rent, rates and insurance	
Van expenses	
Car expenses	
Wages and salaries	
Telephone and office costs	
Diaries	
Parking fines	
Capital allowances	
Taxable profit	

7 BENABI

Benabi's business has the following statement of profit or loss for the year ended 31 March 2022:

	£	£
Turnover		424,800
Less: Cost of sales		(280,900)
Gross profit		143,900
Wages and salaries	67,400	
Rent, rates and insurance	8,100	
Repairs to plant	3,456	
Advertising and entertaining	6,098	
Accountancy and legal costs	2,400	
Motor expenses	5,555	
Depreciation	8,001	
Telephone and office costs	3,699	
Other expenses	5,702	
		(110,411)
Net profit		33,489

Additional information:

1 Wages and salaries include:

	£
Benabi	6,000
Benabi's wife, who works in the marketing department	8,000

2 Advertising and entertaining includes:

	£
Gifts to customers:	
Boxes of chocolates, costing £5 each	1,250
Calendars carrying the business's logo, costing £10 each	400
Staff Christmas party for 8 employees	480

3 Motor expenses include:

	£
Sales manager's car	820
Benabi's car which is only used for private mileage	1,100

4 Other expenses include:

	£
Cost of staff training	490
Subscription to a local gym for Benabi	220

5 Capital allowances have already been calculated at £9,955.

Calculate Benabi's tax adjusted trading profits for the year ended 31 March 2022 using the following pro forma.

Where an item does not require adjustment insert a 0. Where an item is to be deducted from accounting profit, this should be shown as a negative figure, either using a minus sign or brackets.

	£
Accounting profit	33,489
Wages and salaries	
Rent, rates and insurance	
Repairs to plant	
Advertising and entertaining	
Accountancy and legal costs	
Motor expenses	
Depreciation	
Telephone and office costs	
Other expenses	
Capital allowances	
Taxable profit	

8   FRANKLIN LTD

Franklin Ltd commenced to trade on 1 April 2021 and incurred the following expenditure in its first year of trading to 31 March 2022.

(a)   **For each item of expenditure, tick the appropriate box to show whether the item will be treated as allowable or disallowable in the adjustment of trading profits computation.**

	Allowable	Disallowable
Advertising costs incurred in January 2021		
Entertaining prospective customers in February 2021		
Dividends paid to shareholders on 2 January 2022		

Silvain, Alice, Lucille and Pascal have the following trading income and expenses for the year ended 31 March 2022. All expenses were allowable for tax purposes.

	Silvain	Alice	Lucille	Pascal
	£	£	£	£
Trading income	860	690	3,750	6,300
Expenses	300	740	930	3,080

(b)   Complete the following table to show whether each taxpayer should use the trading allowance. Where relevant, show whether the allowance would be given automatically, whether the taxpayer should elect to receive the allowance or whether he/she should elect not to claim the allowance. Calculate the taxable trading income for each taxpayer. Enter 0 if there would be no taxable trading income.

	Silvain	Alice	Lucille	Pascal
Should use the trading allowance				
Given automatically				
Elect to receive				
Elect not to receive				
Taxable trading income (£)				

CAPITAL ALLOWANCES

Key answer tips

Task 2 in the assessment will test capital allowances, which will be partly human marked. This is likely to include a capital allowances computation. You may be required to complete a computation with separate columns dealing with additions qualifying for AIA, for FYA and for the super deduction as appropriate. The answers in this exam kit use this approach of separate columns for these additions.

Therefore, to complete the computation put the opening TWDV figures into the appropriate columns if this has not already been done.

Then put all additions into the appropriate columns, and give the AIA, FYA, super deduction as appropriate. In this exam kit, these additions are added into the appropriate column at cost value and then AIA, FYA, super deduction is claimed as appropriate. However, remember when entering the allowances in the final allowances column, to multiply by 130% in respect of additions qualifying for the super deduction. This is only relevant for companies. You do not need to fill every column – if there are no additions qualifying for AIA, for example, leave this column blank.

Deduct any disposals.

Finally calculate the writing down allowances at 18%/6% on the general pool and the special rate pool.

Make sure you calculate and show a total figure for allowances, and figures for the TWDV carried forward.

You must learn the detailed rules regarding the treatment of different types of asset, especially cars, as you may be assessed on the theory behind the capital allowance rules in a separate part of the task. The Business Tax reference material contains useful information on rates of allowance and limits in the section headed 'Capital allowances'.

You must also be able to deal with short or long accounting periods and the period leading up to the cessation of the business.

9   BROAD LTD

Broad Ltd has the following non-current asset information for the year ended 31 December 2021:

	£
Balances brought forward as at 1 January 2021:	
General pool	140,000
Special rate pool	26,000
Addition in March 2021:	
Plant	10,000
Additions in May and June 2021:	
Machinery	1,020,000
Finance Director's car (Citroen)	34,000
Sales Director's car (BMW)	32,000
Disposals in June 2021:	
Machinery (Cost £10,000)	10,200
Sales Director's car (Vauxhall) (cost £21,000)	13,800

The CO_2 emissions of the car additions are:

Citroen	0g/km
BMW	45g/km

The Vauxhall had been added to the special rate pool when purchased.

All the cars are used 75% for business and 25% privately.

(a)   **Calculate Broad Ltd's total capital allowances and show the balances to carry forward to the next accounting period.**

Use the grid provided for your answer. You have been given more space than you need.

	FYA	AIA	Super deduction	General pool	Special rate pool	Allowances
	£	£	£	£	£	£

Susan is a sole trader and purchased a new building from a developer to use in her trade on 1 September 2021. After furnishing the building, Susan started using it in her trade on 1 December 2021. Susan prepares accounts for the year ended 31 March 2022.

Susan's costs in relation to the building were as follows:

	£
Building cost paid to developer	280,000
Land cost paid to developer	120,000
Office furniture	18,000

(b) (i) **Calculate the amount of expenditure which qualifies for structures and buildings allowance.**

(ii) **Calculate the amount of structures and buildings allowance Susan can claim for the year ended 31 March 2022. State your answer in whole pounds.**

10 WELL LTD

Well Ltd has provided the following information for the year ended 31 March 2022:

	£
Balances brought forward as at 1 April 2021:	
General pool	134,500
Special rate pool	36,000
Additions in May 2021:	
Machinery	644,167
Finance Director's car (Peugeot) (CO$_2$ emissions 42g/km)	34,500
Disposals in September 2021:	
Machinery (Cost £12,000)	10,000
Finance Director's car (Toyota) (Cost £13,200) (which had been included in the special rate pool)	11,800

Both cars are used 40% privately.

(a) **Calculate Well Ltd's total capital allowances and show the balances to carry forward to the next accounting period.**

Use the grid provided for your answer. You have been given more space than you need.

	FYA	AIA	Super deduction	General pool	Special rate pool	Allowances
	£	£	£	£	£	£

Peter is a sole trader. He had a TWDV of £10,000 on his general pool at 1 January 2021 and prepares accounts for the 15-month period ending 31 March 2022. In May 2021 Peter bought a new zero emissions car for £20,000 with 100% business use.

(b) **Explain the capital allowance implications for Peter of the 15-month period ending 31 March 2022.**

11 PINKER LTD

Pinker Ltd changed its accounting date and has sent you the following information about its non-current assets for the five-month accounting period ended 31 May 2021.

Balances brought forward as at 1 January 2021:

General pool	£345,980
Special rate pool	£23,000

In January 2021 the company bought plant for £539,000. In April 2021 the company bought a car with CO2 emissions of 43g/km for £18,000, and a car with zero emissions for £13,790.

(a) **Calculate Pinker Ltd's total capital allowances and show the balances to carry forward to the next accounting period.**

Use the grid provided for your answer. You have been given more space than you need.

	FYA	AIA	Super deduction	General pool	Special rate pool	Allowances
	£	£	£	£	£	£

(b)   **Select whether each of the following statements about the structures and buildings allowance in respect of a building is true or false.**

	True	False
The allowance for a year is 3% of the brought forward tax written down value of the building		
The allowance is time apportioned if the building was brought into use part way through the year		
Expenditure on land does not qualify for the allowance		
If the building is sold to a second user, the allowance for the second user is 3% of the price paid by the second user		
The allowance is available to both companies and unincorporated businesses		

12   SARAH

Sarah's sole trader business has the following non-current asset information for the year ended 31 December 2021:

	£
Balances brought forward as at 1 January 2021:	
General pool	65,100
Sarah's Peugeot car (20% private usage) – special rate	14,500
Additions in July 2021:	
Office furniture	11,000
Van	8,600
Sarah's Toyota car – to be used solely for business purposes	20,000
Plant	15,500
Disposals:	
Office furniture – original cost higher than disposal value	14,200
Sarah's Peugeot car	10,000

The CO_2 emissions of the vehicles are:

Van   130g/km

Toyota   0g/km

Calculate Sarah's total capital allowances and show the balances to carry forward to the next accounting period.

Use the grid provided for your answer. You have been given more space than you need.

	AIA	FYA	General pool	Special rate pool	Private use asset	Allowances
	£	£	£	£	£	£

(b) **Identify which of the following statements about the structures and buildings allowance is correct.**

A   Costs of obtaining planning permission are qualifying expenditure

B   The rate of the allowance is 6%

C   The allowance is not available if a building is bought second-hand

D   The allowance is time apportioned for a short accounting period

Lleaff Ltd prepares accounts for the year ended 31 March 2022. It purchased new plant on 1 January 2022.

(c) **Identify which of the following statements about the capital allowances available on the plant is correct.**

A   The maximum annual investment allowance available is £250,000

B   A super deduction of 130% of the expenditure is available

C   A writing down allowance limited to 18% × 3/12 of the expenditure is available

D   A first year allowance of 100% of the expenditure is available

13   DAVE AND NICK

Dave and Nick formed a partnership and started trading on 1 January 2021.

The partnership made the following non-current asset additions in the period ended 31 August 2021:

	£
Plant – January 2021	7,680
Office furniture – January 2021	12,450
Car for Dave, 30% private use, CO_2 emissions 105g/km – April 2021	15,300
Car for Nick, 40% private use, CO_2 emissions 40g/km – April 2021	10,200

(a)   (i)   Calculate the partnership's total capital allowances and show the balances to carry forward to the next accounting period.

Use the grid provided for your answer. You have been given more space than you need.

	FYA	AIA	General pool	Special rate pool	Private use asset 1	Private use asset 2	Allowances
	£	£	£	£	£	£	£

The partnership did not do well and ceased to trade on 31 March 2022. Further plant had been bought in September 2021 costing £10,000.

When the trade ceased all the plant and furniture was sold for £22,000. Dave and Nick took over their cars at market value of £12,500 and £7,500 respectively.

(ii) Calculate the partnership's total capital allowances for the final period of trading.

Use the grid provided for your answer. You have been given more space than you need.

	FYA	AIA	General pool	Special rate pool	Private use asset 1	Private use asset 2	Allowances
	£	£	£	£	£	£	£

(b) Indicate whether the following statement about the super deduction is true or false.

The super deduction is available on the purchase of plant and buildings on or after 1 April 2021 by a company

	True	False

14   PIRBRIGHT LTD

Pirbright Ltd has the following non-current asset information for the year ended 30 June 2021:

			£
Balances brought forward as at 1 July 2020:			
General pool			81,000
Special rate pool			28,900
Additions:			
1 March 2021	Machinery		640,000
1 May 2021	New equipment		50,000
11 May 2021	New Hyundai car		21,000
1 June 2021	Managing Director's Jaguar car		38,600
Disposals:			
26 February 2021	Machinery	Cost £22,000	11,250
1 June 2021	Managing Director's Lexus car	Cost £30,000	15,400

The CO_2 emissions of the vehicles are:

Hyundai   0g/km

Jaguar   82g/km

The Lexus had been included in the special rate pool.

The Managing Director used the Jaguar and Lexus 30% privately.

(a)   Calculate Pirbright Ltd's total capital allowances and show the balances to carry forward to the next accounting period.

Use the grid provided for your answer. You have been given more space than you need.

	FYA	AIA	Super deduction	General pool	Special rate pool	Allowances
	£	£	£	£	£	£

Shirin is a sole trader. She purchased a new machine for £300,000 in January 2022. She made no other purchases during the three-month period ended 31 March 2022.

(b)   Explain the capital allowance available on the purchase of the new machine.

15 AMOLI

Amoli's sole trader business has the following non-current asset information for the 15 month period ended 31 March 2022:

	£
Balances brought forward as at 1 January 2021:	
General pool	23,400
Amoli's petrol car (30% private usage) – special rate	8,700
Additions in May 2021:	
Amoli's new electric car (30% private usage)	30,000
Machinery	15,000
Van CO_2 emissions 185g/km	25,000
Car for use by employee (40% private use) CO_2 emissions 45g/km	20,000
Disposals in May 2021:	
Packaging equipment (bought for £12,000)	13,100
Amoli's petrol car (proceeds less than cost)	11,000

(a) **Calculate Amoli's total capital allowances and show the balances to carry forward to the next accounting period.**

Use the grid provided for your answer. You have been given more space than you need.

	AIA	FYA	General pool	Special rate pool	Private use asset	Allowances
	£	£	£	£	£	£

Twigg Ltd paid for the construction of a new head office. The land cost £500,000 and the costs of construction were £1,500,000. Twigg Ltd incurred costs of £2,000 in respect of planning permission. In June 2021 Twigg Ltd fits out the offices with furniture costing £75,000.

Twigg Ltd started using the office on 1 July 2021.

(b)   Identify which ONE of the following statements about the purchase is true.

A   The structures and buildings allowance for the year ended 31 December 2021 is 3% of qualifying expenditure

B   The maximum allowance available in respect of the furniture is £75,000

C   The cost of the land does not qualify for any allowance

D   The cost of the planning permission qualifies for the structures and buildings allowance

Liam is a sole trader. He has a tax written down value of £4,000 on the general pool and a tax written down value £5,000 in respect of a car, car A. Liam sold car A and another car, car B during the year ended 31 March 2022.

Car A had been used by Liam for 70% business use and was sold for £6,000. Car B which had zero emissions, had been used by an employee with 40% private use, and was sold for £1,000. Both cars were sold for less than their cost.

(c)   **Explain the treatment of the disposals for capital allowances purposes.**

BASIS PERIOD RULES

Key answer tips

Basis of assessment for new, ongoing and ceasing businesses as well as partnerships (see the next section) is an important topic and will be tested in Task 3 of the assessment. This task may be broken into a number of smaller tasks rather than one large one.

These rules are covered in the Business Tax reference material provided in your assessment in the section headed 'Income tax basis period rules'.

It is important to use an appropriate amount of time in the assessment for these tasks, and not to rush your answer.

16   KURT

Kurt started trading on 1 October 2018. He prepares his accounts to 30 June each year.

His tax adjusted trading profits were calculated as follows:

	£
Period to 30 June 2019	22,500
Year to 30 June 2020	43,200
Year to 30 June 2021	47,000

(a)   **The tax year in which he started trading was:**

A   2017/18

B   2018/19

C   2019/20

D   2020/21

(b)   **His taxable profits in his first tax year of trading were:**

A   £15,000

B   £15,750

C   £22,500

D   £17,500

(c)   **His taxable profits in his second tax year of trading were:**

A   £43,200

B   £39,900

C   £33,300

D   £22,500

(d)   **His taxable profits in his third tax year of trading were:**

A   £47,000

B   £43,200

C   £44,150

D   £46,050

(e)   **His overlap profits were:**

(f)   **Indicate whether the following statement about Kurt's choice of accounting date is true or false.**

	True	False
If Kurt had chosen an accounting date of 31 December rather than 30 June, his overlap profits would have been greater		

17   ROBERT

Robert started trading on 1 January 2020. He prepares his accounts to 31 October each year.

His tax adjusted trading profits were calculated as follows:

	£
10 months to 31 October 2020	32,000
Year ended 31 October 2021	45,000
Year ended 31 October 2022	87,000

(a)   (i)   **His taxable profits for 2019/20 were:**

A   £32,000

B   £9,600

C   £39,500

D   £45,000

(ii)   **His taxable profits for 2020/21 were:**

A   £32,000

B   £45,000

C   £39,500

D   £41,150

(iii) **His taxable profits for 2021/22 will be:**

A   £32,000

B   £45,000

C   £87,000

D   £62,500

(iv) **His overlap profits were:**

[   ]

Cerys ceased to trade on 30 September 2021. She previously prepared accounts to 30 June each year. Her final period of accounts is for the three months ended 30 September 2021.

She has overlap profits of £3,000 from starting trade.

(b) **Indicate whether the following statements are true or false.**

	True	False
Cerys' basis period for 2021/22 is the 15 month period from 1 July 2020 to 30 September 2021		
Cerys' assessable profits for 2021/22 will be increased by the overlap profits of £3,000		

18   JAVID

Javid starts trading on 1 January 2021 and draws up his first set of accounts to 31 May 2022. The profits for the period are £34,000.

(a) **(i)** **The tax year in which Javid first started trading was:**

A   2019/20

B   2020/21

C   2021/22

D   2022/23

(ii) **The assessable profits for the first year of trade are:**

A   £6,000

B   £8,500

C   £24,000

D   £34,000

(iii) **The period for which his profits will be assessed for the second tax year will be:**

A   1 January 2021 to 5 April 2021

B   1 January 2021 to 31 December 2021

C   6 April 2021 to 5 April 2022

D   12 months to 31 May 2022

      (iv)   **The overlap profits are:**

          A   £6,000

          B   £8,500

          C   £20,000

          D   £24,000

(b)   **Indicate whether the following statements are true or false.**

	True	False
An accounting date of 31 March means no overlap profits arise		
An accounting date of 31 March maximises the delay between generating profits and paying tax on those profits		

19   CHARIS

Charis commenced business as a sole trader on 1 January 2021 and prepared her first set of accounts for the period ended 28 February 2022.

In the 14-month period ended 28 February 2022 her tax adjusted trading profits were £21,000.

Her second set of accounts will be for the year ended 28 February 2023, when the tax adjusted trading profits are expected to be £24,000.

(a)   **The tax year in which Charis started trading was:**

      A   2019/20

      B   2020/21

      C   2021/22

      D   2022/23

(b)   **Her assessable profits in her second year of trading are:**

(c)   **Her assessable profits in her third year of trading are:**

(d)   **Her overlap profits from commencement of trade are:**

(e)   **Indicate whether the following statements are true or false for Charis.**

	True	False
If Charis had chosen an accounting date of March instead of February, overlap profits would be nil.		
When Charis ceases to trade, the overlap profits will increase her taxable profits in the last year of trade.		

20 GORDON

Gordon ceased trading on 30 November 2021.

Until then, he had been preparing his accounts to 30 June each year.

The tax adjusted trading profits in the final periods of trading were as follows:

	£
Year to 30 June 2020	132,000
Year to 30 June 2021	120,000
Period to 30 November 2021	56,000

He had overlap profits from commencement of trade of £22,000.

(a) **The tax year in which he ceased trading was:**

A   2019/20

B   2020/21

C   2021/22

D   2022/23

(b) **His taxable profits in his penultimate tax year of trading were:**

A   £132,000

B   £120,000

C   £56,000

D   £123,000

(c) **His taxable profits in his final tax year of trading were:**

A   £176,000

B   £154,000

C   £34,000

D   £56,000

(d) **His overlap profits remaining after cessation are:**

(e) **Indicate whether the following statements are true or false if Gordon had used a 30 September accounting date rather than 30 June.**

	True	False
His overlap profits from commencement would have been lower		
The total profits taxed over the lifetime of the business would have been lower		

21   HENRIETTA

Henrietta started trading on 1 February 2020. She prepares her first set of accounts to 31 May 2021 and then to 31 May each year.

Her tax adjusted trading profits were calculated as follows:

	£
Period to 31 May 2021	7,860
Year to 31 May 2022	8,820
Year to 31 May 2023	15,000

(a)   **The tax year in which she started trading was:**

A   2021/22

B   2018/19

C   2019/20

D   2020/21

(b)   **Her taxable profits in her first tax year of trading were:**

A   £7,860

B   £3,930

C   £983

D   £5,895

(c)   **Her taxable profits in her second tax year of trading were:**

A   £5,895

B   £7,860

C   £8,820

D   £6,877

(d)   **Her taxable profits in her third tax year of trading were:**

A   £15,000

B   £5,895

C   £8,820

D   £8,333

(e)   **Her overlap profits were:**

[   ]

(f)   **If Henrietta had chosen an accounting date to 31 August instead of 31 May, select which one of the following statements is true.**

A   Overlap profits would be greater

B   Overlap profits would be lower.

22 MELISSA

Melissa ceased trading on 30 June 2022.

Until then, she had been preparing her accounts to 30 September each year.

The tax adjusted trading profits in the final periods of trading were as follows:

	£
Year to 30 September 2020	13,000
Year to 30 September 2021	12,000
Period to 30 June 2022	5,000

She had overlap profits from commencement of trade of £2,000.

(a) **(i)** **The tax year in which Melissa ceased trading was:**

(ii) **Her taxable profits in her penultimate tax year of trading were:**

(iii) **Her taxable profits in her final tax year of trading were:**

Jimmy started to trade on 1 March 2021.

(b) **Indicate whether the following statements are true or false for Jimmy.**

	True	False
Jimmy's first year of trade is 2021/22.		
If Jimmy prepares his first set of accounts for the year ended 28 February 2022, he will have overlap profits of 1/12 of his first year's profits.		
If Jimmy wishes to delay the payment of tax on his profits for as long as possible, he should choose an accounting date of 30 April.		

ANALYSING PROFITS AND LOSSES OF A PARTNERSHIP AND CALCULATING NICS

Key answer tips

In Task 4 of the assessment you may be asked to complete a table to show the apportionment of profit to partners. Some of the entries in the table may already be completed. The totals may be calculated automatically but if not, you should complete these if there is space for these. You should only enter your answers in the table, not workings.

Only classes 2 and 4 NICs are assessable; however, you may be asked to calculate the NICs payable by sole traders or partners.

The Business Tax reference material provided in your assessment covers this topic in the section headed 'National insurance (NI)'.

23   **SUE, WILL AND TERRI**

Sue and Will have been in partnership for many years, preparing their accounts to 30 September each year. Their profit sharing ratio was 3:2 respectively.

On 1 April 2021, Terri joined the partnership and the profit sharing ratio was changed to 2:2:1 for Sue, Will and Terri.

For the year ended 30 September 2021, the tax adjusted trading profit was £84,000.

(a)   Calculate the trading profits apportioned to each partner for the year ended 30 September 2021, completing the table. Enter 0 (zero) if the answer is nil and enter answers in whole pounds.

	Sue	Will	Terri	Total
	£	£	£	£
Period to 31 March 2021				
Profit share				
Period to 30 September 2021				
Profit share				
Total				

Jenny has trading income from self-employment of £85,000 for 2021/22 of which she took drawings of £65,000.

(b)   **The amount of class 4 NICs payable (to the nearest pence) is:**   £

Jack has trading income from self-employment of £25,000 for 2021/22.

(c)   **The amount of class 2 NICs payable (to the nearest pence) is:**   £

24 JENNY AND HARVEY

Jenny and Harvey are in partnership, and have always shared profits equally.

It was then decided that from 1 April 2021 Jenny would be awarded a salary of £40,000 per annum to recognise the extra work that she had taken on.

For the year ended 31 December 2021, the tax adjusted trading profits of the partnership were £150,000.

(a) **Calculate the trading profits apportioned to each partner for the year ended 31 December 2021, completing the table. Enter 0 (zero) if the answer is nil and enter answers in whole pounds.**

	Jenny	Harvey	Total
	£	£	£
Period to 31 March 2021			
Salary			
Profit share			
Total for period			
Period to 31 December 2021			
Salary			
Profit share			
Total for period			
Total for year			

Ivor's share of his partnership's taxable trading income is £100,000 for 2021/22. He also received salary of £10,000 from a director role.

(b) (i) **The amount chargeable to class 4 NICs at 9% is:**   £

(ii) **The amount chargeable to class 4 NICs at 2% is:**   £

(iii) **The amount of class 2 NICs payable (to the nearest pence) is:**   £

25 SALLY, BARRY, BILL AND BEA

Sally, Barry, Bill and Bea have been in partnership for many years, preparing their accounts to 31 May each year. Their profit sharing ratio was 4:2:2:1 respectively after allowing 5% p.a. interest on capital.

On 1 September 2020, they changed the profit sharing ratio to 4:3:2:2 for Sally, Barry, Bill and Bea respectively and decided to have no more interest on capital.

For the year ended 31 May 2021, the partnership's tax adjusted trading profit was £756,000.

The partner's capital balances at the start of the period of account were £80,000, £100,000, £200,000 and £90,000 for Sally, Barry, Bill and Bea respectively.

(a) **Show the division of profit for each of the partners for the year ended 31 May 2021, completing the table. Enter 0 (zero) if the answer is nil and enter answers in whole pounds.**

	Sally	Barry	Bill	Bea	Total
	£	£	£	£	£
Period to 31 August 2020					
Interest on capital					
Profit share					
Total for period					
Period to 31 May 2021					
Interest on capital					
Profit share					
Total for period					
Total					756,000

Jake's sole trader business has made a taxable trading profit of £60,000 for 2021/22.

(b) **The amount of class 2 NICs payable by Jake (to the nearest pence) for the year is:**   £ _____

Sue has taxable trading profits of £41,000 for 2021/22.

(c) **The amount of total class 4 NICs payable by Sue (to the nearest pence) is:**   £ _____

26 ALVIN, SIMON AND THEODORE

Alvin, Simon and Theodore have been in partnership for many years, preparing their accounts to 31 January each year. Their profit sharing ratio was 5:3:2 respectively.

On 1 August 2021, Theodore retired from the partnership and the profit sharing ratio was changed to 1:1 for Alvin and Simon.

For the year ended 31 January 2022, the tax adjusted trading profit was £52,800.

(a) **Calculate the trading profits apportioned to each partner for the year ended 31 January 2022, completing the table. Complete the dates for each period end. Enter 0 (zero) if the answer is nil and enter answers in whole pounds.**

	Alvin	Simon	Theodore	Total
	£	£	£	£
Period to _____				
Profit share				
Period to _____				
Profit share				
Total				

Thomas received a state pension of £6,980 throughout 2021/22 and had self-employed income of £55,000 for 2021/22.

(b) **The amount chargeable to class 4 NICs at 9% is:** £

Suzanne, aged 42, has self-employed income of £35,000 for 2021/22.

(c) **The amount of total class 4 NICs payable (to the nearest pence) is:** £

27 SIAN AND ELLIE

Sian and Ellie have been in partnership for many years, preparing their accounts to 31 July each year. Their profit sharing ratio was 2:1 respectively.

On 1 May 2021, Owen joined the partnership and the profit sharing ratio was changed to 3:2:1 for Sian, Ellie and Owen respectively.

The tax adjusted trading profit was £36,000 for the year ended 31 July 2021, and £60,000 for the year ended 31 July 2022.

(a) **(i)** **Calculate the trading profits apportioned to each partner for the year ended 31 July 2021 and for the year ended 31 July 2022, completing the table. Complete the dates for each period end. Enter 0 (zero) if the answer is nil and enter answers in whole pounds.**

	Sian	Ellie	Owen	Total
	£	£	£	£
Period to 30 April 2021				
Profit share				
Period to 31 July 2021				
Profit share				
Total for y/e 31 July 2021				
Total for y/e 31 July 2022				

(ii) **Calculate Owen's assessable profits for 2021/22 and 2022/23.**

2021/22   £

2022/23   £

Amelie and Alexander are in partnership sharing profits in the ratio 60:40 after paying a salary of £5,000 to Alexander. The partnership's taxable trading profit for the year ended 31 March 2022 was £75,000.

(b) **(i)** **The amount of class 4 NICs payable by Amelie (to the nearest pence) is:** £

(ii) **The amount of class 4 NICs payable by Alexander (to the nearest pence) is:** £

(iii) **The amount of class 2 NICs payable by Amelie (to the nearest pence) is:** £

28   NOEL, DAVID AND LUCY

Noel, David and Lucy have been in partnership for many years, preparing their accounts to 31 March each year. Their profit sharing ratio was 1:3:2 respectively.

On 1 January 2022, Lucy left the partnership. From that date David received a salary of £16,000 per annum and the profit sharing ratio was changed to 1:1 for Noel and David.

For the year ended 31 March 2022, the partnership made a loss of £80,000.

(a)   Calculate the trading loss apportioned to each partner for the year ended 31 March 2022, completing the table. Enter loss figures as negative amounts using brackets. Enter 0 (zero) if the answer is nil and enter answers in whole pounds.

	Noel	David	Lucy	Total
	£	£	£	£
Period to 31 December 2021				
Salary				
Loss share				
Period to 31 March 2022				
Salary				
Loss share				
Total for the year				(80,000)

Anj has partnership trading income of £70,000 for 2021/22.

(b)   (i)   The amount of class 4 NICs payable at 9% (to the nearest pence) is: £ ____

(ii)   The amount of class 4 NICs payable at 2% (to the nearest pence) is: £ ____

(iii)   The total amount of class 4 NICs payable (to the nearest pence) is: £ ____

Pete's partnership trading profit is £4,000 for 2021/22.

(c)   The total amount of NICs payable by Pete (to the nearest pence) is: £ ____

29   TOMMY, GRACE AND BRIDIE

Tommy and Grace have been in partnership for many years, preparing their accounts to 31 March each year. Their profit sharing ratio was 4:1 respectively.

On 1 October 2021, Bridie joined the partnership. From that date, Tommy and Grace received annual salaries of £20,000 each and the profit sharing ratio was changed to 2:1:1 for Tommy, Grace and Bridie respectively.

The tax adjusted trading profit of the partnership was £200,000 for the year ended 31 March 2022.

(a)   Calculate the trading profits/losses apportioned to each partner for the year ended 31 March 2022, completing the table. Complete the dates for each period end. Enter 0 (zero) if the answer is nil and enter answers in whole pounds.

	Tommy	**Grace**	**Bridie**	**Total**
	£	£	£	£
Period to 30 September 2021				
Salary				
Profit share				
Period to 31 March 2022				
Salary				
Profit share				
Total for y/e 31 March 2022				

Sunil has trading income from self-employment of £62,000 for 2021/22.

(b) **The amount of class 4 NICs payable (to the nearest pence) is:** £

Kat has trading income from self-employment of £8,000 for 2021/22.

(c) **The amount of class 2 NICs payable (to the nearest pence) is:** £

CHARGEABLE GAINS AND ALLOWABLE LOSSES OF COMPANIES

Key answer tips

Task 5 of the assessment tests the calculation of chargeable gains and allowable losses on disposals by companies. For expenditure incurred before December 2017 the indexation allowance is available to reduce a gain.

You may also be asked about rollover relief which reduces chargeable gains for individuals and companies, but this relief will only be examined in questions involving companies.

The Business Tax reference material provided in your assessment covers rollover relief in the section headed 'Chargeable gains – Reliefs'.

30 WENDYCO LTD

(a) **Select whether the following statements are true or false.**

Tick the appropriate box for each statement.

	True	**False**
Indexation allowance cannot create an allowable capital loss		
If not all proceeds on the sale of an asset are reinvested in a new asset, the rollover relief will be equal to the amount of proceeds not reinvested		
Rollover relief claimed when an old building is sold and a new building bought reduces the base cost of the new building		

Wendyco Ltd sold a factory building for £500,000 in May 2021.

Wendyco Ltd bought the factory for £120,000 in January 2000. In June 2015, the company spent £80,000 on an extension and redecorated the existing part of the building for £20,000.

The indexation factor from January 2000 to December 2017 was 0.669.

The indexation factor from June 2015 to December 2017 was 0.074.

(b)   Complete the following computation of Wendyco Ltd's chargeable gain. Show deductions as negative figures.

	£
Sale proceeds	
Cost	
Enhancement expenditure	
Indexation allowance	
Chargeable gain	

31   XYZ LTD

XYZ Ltd sold a building for £250,000 in January 2022.

The building was purchased for £100,000 in April 2009. An extension was built at a cost of £22,000 in May 2013.

In June 2017 repairs to the roof tiles were made costing £12,000

The indexation factor from April 2009 to December 2017 was 0.315

The indexation factor from May 2013 to December 2017 was 0.112

The indexation factor from June 2017 to December 2017 was 0.021

(a)   Complete the following computation of the chargeable gain for XYZ Ltd:

	£
Sale proceeds	
Costs	
Indexation allowance	
Chargeable gain/allowable loss	

(b) **Select whether the following statements are true or false.**

Tick the appropriate box for each statement.

	True	False
For rollover relief to be available on the sale of a building, a new building must be bought		
Rollover relief cannot create a loss		

32 TOPHAM LTD

Topham Ltd sold a piece of land for £42,000 in November 2021.

The land was bought for £40,000 in September 2014.

The indexation factor from September 2014 to December 2017 was 0.080.

(a) **Complete the following computation:**

	£
Sale proceeds	
Cost	
Indexation allowance	
Chargeable gain/allowable loss	

(b) **Select whether the following statements about rollover relief are true or false.**

Tick the appropriate box for each statement.

	True	False
The relief is available on a sale of a qualifying asset if a qualifying replacement asset is bought within three years before or after the sale		
The base cost of a replacement building is reduced by the relief claimed		
The relief is not available on the sale of a building which has always been rented out		

33 MALLC LTD

Mallc Ltd bought a warehouse for £350,000 in March 2011.

In June 2021, it was sold for £725,000.

In the same month the company bought a factory for £590,000.

The indexation factor from March 2011 to December 2017 was 0.196.

(a) **Complete the following for Mallc Ltd:**

The gain chargeable before rollover relief is:

£ _____

The gain chargeable after rollover relief is:

£ _____

The amount of rollover relief is:

£ _____

The base cost of the factory is:

£ _____

Jerme Ltd sold a qualifying business asset on 1 September 2021, during its accounting period ended 31 December 2021.

(b) **The dates during which the proceeds must be reinvested in another qualifying business asset to be eligible for rollover relief are between:**

A		B
	and	

Choose one date from each of the options below and insert in the appropriate place in the table above.

Options:

A   1 September 2021; 1 September 2018; 1 January 2021; 31 December 2020; 1 September 2020

B   31 December 2021; 31 December 2022; 1 September 2022; 1 September 2023; 1 September 2024

34   OLIVER LTD

A factory was sold by Oliver Ltd for £800,000 in May 2021. Oliver Ltd had purchased the factory for £300,000 in January 2002 and had built an extension for £100,000 in June 2019.

Oliver Ltd purchased a warehouse in January 2022 for £750,000.

The indexation factor from January 2002 to December 2017 was 0.605

(a) (i)   **Calculate the unindexed gain before rollover relief.**

_____

(ii) **Calculate the indexation allowance.**

_____

(iii) **Calculate the rollover relief.**

_____

(iv)   Select whether the following statements for Oliver Ltd are true or false. For each item, assume this is the only change from the scenario above.

Tick the appropriate box for each statement.

	True	False
If the warehouse had been purchased in January 2021 rollover relief would have been available.		
If Oliver Ltd had instead purchased fixed plant rather than the warehouse, rollover relief would have been available.		
If Oliver Ltd had instead invested in shares in an unquoted trading company, rollover relief would have been available.		

35   ALLYNN LTD

Allynn Ltd bought fixed plant for £1,400,000 in January 2014.

In November 2021, the plant was sold for £2,850,000.

In the same month a factory was bought for £2,000,000.

The indexation factor from January 2014 to December 2017 was 0.101.

(a)   **Complete the following:**

The gain chargeable before rollover relief is: £

The amount of rollover relief is: £

The base cost of the factory is: £

Simon Ltd sold a qualifying business asset on 1 February 2020. Simon Ltd prepares accounts to 31 March each year.

(b)   **The dates during which the proceeds must be reinvested in another qualifying business asset to be eligible for rollover relief are between:**

A	and	B

Choose one date from each of the options below and insert in the appropriate place in the table above.

Options:

A   1 February 2019; 1 April 2019; 1 February 2017; 31 March 2019; 31 March 2020

B   1 February 2020; 31 March 2020; 1 February 2021; 31 March 2023; 1 February 2022; 1 February 2023

36 CHERY LTD

Chery Ltd sold an office building used in its trade for £3,800,000 in February 2022. Chery Ltd paid legal fees on the sale of £7,000. The purchaser paid legal fees of £6,000.

Chery Ltd had bought the building for £2,600,000 in January 2018, and paid legal fees of £3,000 in the same month. The building was in a state of disrepair when purchased and had no roof. Chery Ltd paid for a roof in January 2018 for £250,000.

In March 2021, Chery Ltd painted the windows of the building at a cost of £25,000. The same month, the company paid for repairs to the damp proofing of the building for £56,000.

(a) **Complete the following calculations relating to the chargeable gain for Chery Ltd in the year ended 31 March 2022. Enter 0 (zero) if the answer is nil.**

(i) **Calculate the allowable costs of sale.**

(ii) **Calculate the allowable costs incurred in January 2018.**

(iii) **Calculate the allowable enhancement expenditure in March 2021.**

(iv) **Select whether the following statements are true or false, in relation to Chery Ltd above.**

Tick the appropriate box for each statement.

	True	False
Indexation allowance is available on the costs of purchase from January 2018 to February 2022.		
If a replacement office building were bought for £4,000,000 in March 2022 and let out, full rollover relief would be available.		
If a warehouse had been bought for £3,600,000 in May 2021 for use in the trade, partial rollover relief would be available.		

CALCULATING CHARGEABLE GAINS AND ALLOWABLE LOSSES IN COMPANY DISPOSAL OF SHARES

Key answer tips

Task 6 will cover disposals of shares by a company. This task is humanly marked and will include a share pool, which may include a combination of purchases, disposals, bonus issues and rights issues. You must then calculate the gain. The question is likely to be complex with a number of different transactions.

Be careful to remember the matching rules – not all disposals will necessarily be matched with the share pool, therefore it is important to consider these rules first.

37   PUCK LTD

Puck Ltd prepares accounts to 31 March each year.

Puck Ltd bought 3,000 shares in Quinn Ltd in June 2008 for £12,000.

In January 2012, there was a 1 for 3 bonus issue and in December 2015 there was a 1 for 4 rights issue at £2 a share.

All shares were sold in April 2021 for £24,000.

Indexation factors were:

	January 2012	December 2015	December 2017
June 2008	0.098	0.202	
January 2012		0.095	
December 2015			0.067

(a)   Complete the share pool for the Quinn Ltd shares. Include the carried forward amounts. Enter amounts in whole pounds.

Transaction	Number of shares	Cost	Indexed cost
		£	£

(b)   **Calculate the chargeable gain or allowable loss on disposal of the Quinn Ltd shares in the year ended 31 March 2022. Enter amounts in whole pounds.**

38   PISTON LTD

Piston Ltd prepares accounts for the year ended 31 December 2021.

Piston Ltd sold all of its ordinary shares in Power plc for £18,800 on 12 May 2021.

Piston Ltd acquired its shares in Power plc as follows:

10 August 2006	Purchased 2,700 shares for £10,640
19 July 2013	Took up a 1 for 3 bonus issue
20 January 2014	Purchased 2,300 shares for £7,130

Indexation factors were:

August 2006 – July 2013	0.254
August 2006 – January 2014	0.268
July 2013 – January 2014	0.012
January 2014 – December 2017	0.101

(a) Complete the share pool for the Power plc shares. Include the carried forward amounts. Enter amounts in whole pounds.

Transaction	Number of shares	Cost	Indexed cost
		£	£

(b)   Calculate the chargeable gain or allowable on disposal of the Power plc shares in the year ended 31 December 2021. Enter amounts in whole pounds.

39   DREAM LTD

Dream Ltd bought 6,000 shares in Boat Ltd for £12,000 in March 2000.

In June 2005 there was a bonus issue of 1 for 2.

In January 2012, Dream Ltd sold 1,000 shares for £3,000.

In December 2021, 7,000 shares were sold for £46,350.

Dream Ltd prepared accounts for the year ended 31 December 2021.

Indexation factors were:

March 2000 to June 2005	0.141
March 2000 to January 2012	0.413
March 2000 to December 2017	0.651
June 2005 to January 2012	0.238
June 2005 to December 2017	0.447
January 2012 to December 2017	0.168

(a)   Complete the share pool for the Boat Ltd shares. Include the carried forward amounts. Enter amounts in whole pounds.

Transaction	Number of shares	Cost	Indexed cost
		£	£
March 2000	6,000	12,000	12,000

(b) **Calculate the chargeable gain or allowable on disposal of the Boat Ltd shares in the year ended 31 December 2021. Enter amounts in whole pounds.**

40 BATMAN LTD

Batman Ltd bought 7,000 shares in Robin Ltd for £14,000 in May 2006.

It obtained additional shares through a 1 for 8 bonus issue in July 2008 and a 1 for 5 rights issue in July 2012. The rights issue shares were purchased for £3 each.

In September 2021, Batman Ltd sold 5,000 of the shares for £5 per share.

Batman Ltd prepared accounts for the year ended 31 March 2022.

Indexation factors were:

May 2006 to July 2008	0.095
July 2008 to July 2012	0.118
May 2006 to July 2012	0.225
July 2012 to December 2017	0.149

(a)   Complete the share pool for the Robin Ltd shares. Include the carried forward amounts. Enter amounts in whole pounds.

Transaction	Number of shares	Cost	Indexed cost
		£	£

(b) **Calculate the chargeable gain or allowable on disposal of the Robin Ltd shares in the year ended 31 March 2022. Enter amounts in whole pounds.**

41 SHELBYVILLE LTD

On 14 May 2017, Shelbyville Ltd bought 10,000 shares in Springfield plc for £23,300.

On 10 November 2017, Springfield plc issued bonus shares of 1 for 40.

On 29 January 2022, Shelbyville Ltd bought a further 2,000 shares in Springfield plc for £5,950.

On 2 February 2022, Shelbyville Ltd sold 5,875 of these shares for £3.20 each.

Shelbyville Ltd prepared accounts for the year ended 31 March 2022.

Indexation factors were:

May 2017 to November 2017	0.015
May 2017 to December 2017	0.024

(a) Complete the share pool for the Springfield plc shares. Include the carried forward amounts. Enter amounts in whole pounds.

Transaction	Number of shares	Cost	Indexed cost
		£	£

(b) **Calculate the chargeable gain or allowable on disposal of the Springfield plc shares in the year ended 31 March 2022. Enter amounts in whole pounds.**

42 TREACOL LTD

Treacol Ltd prepares accounts for the year ended 30 September 2021.

Treacol Ltd sold 4,000 shares in Syrip Ltd for £32,000 on 8 August 2021.

Treacol Ltd acquired its shares in Syrip Ltd as follows:

5 May 2012	Purchased 5,000 shares for £24,000
7 January 2016	Took up a 1 for 2 rights issue at £6 per share
2 August 2021	Purchased 1,000 shares for £7,800

Indexation factors were:

May 2012 – January 2016	0.068
May 2012 – December 2017	0.147
January 2016 – December 2017	0.075

(a) **Complete the share pool for the Syrip Ltd shares. Include the carried forward amounts. Enter amounts in whole pounds.**

Transaction	Number of shares	Cost	Indexed cost
		£	£

(b)   **Calculate the chargeable gain or allowable on disposal of the Syrip Ltd shares in the year ended 30 September 2021. Enter amounts in whole pounds.**

43   MAPPEL LTD

Mappel Ltd bought 8,000 shares in Trunck Ltd for £36,000 in January 2004.

It bought an additional 2,000 shares for £12,000 in June 2010.

In February 2012, there was a bonus issue of 1 for 4.

In January 2019, Mappel Ltd sold 5,000 shares for £41,000.

In June 2021, a further 3,000 shares were sold for £37,300.

Mappel Ltd prepared accounts for the year ended 30 September 2021.

Indexation factors were:

January 2004 to June 2010	0.224
January 2004 to December 2017	0.519
June 2010 to February 2012	0.071
June 2010 to December 2017	0.241
February 2012 to December 2017	0.159

(a)   Complete the share pool for the Trunck Ltd shares. Include the carried forward amounts. Enter amounts in whole pounds.

Transaction	Number of shares	Cost	Indexed cost
		£	£
January 2004	8,000	36,000	36,000

(b) Calculate the chargeable gain or allowable on disposal of the Trunck Ltd shares in the year ended 30 September 2021. Enter amounts in whole pounds.

CALCULATING TAXABLE PROFITS AND CORPORATION TAX PAYABLE

Key answer tips

Task 7 in the assessment will cover the calculation of taxable total profits and corporation tax payable.

The rate of corporation tax is given in the Business Tax reference material provided in your assessment in the section headed 'Corporation tax'.

Questions on corporation tax payment dates are included in the administrative requirements section of this exam kit.

44 WITHERS LTD

Withers Ltd prepared accounts for the year ended 31 December 2021.

The trading profit before capital allowances was £2,490,000.

The company had bank interest income in the year of £3,000 and dividend income of £50,000.

Property income of £110,000 was receivable from a building rented out by the company. The building was sold on 1 December 2021, giving rise to a chargeable gain of £230,000.

On 31 December 2021 Withers Ltd made a donation to charity of £20,000.

The finance director has calculated capital allowances of £130,000.

Calculate Withers Ltd's taxable total profits and corporation tax payable for the year ended 31 December 2021, completing the table below. Enter 0 (zero) if an amount is nil and show a deduction as a negative figure.

	£
Trading income	
Investment income	
Property income	
Chargeable gains	
Qualifying charitable donations	
Taxable total profits	
Corporation tax payable	

45   MORGAN LTD

Morgan Ltd draws up a 15 month set of accounts to 31 March 2022.

(a)   **Select the corporation tax computations that will need to be prepared.**

A   One computation for the whole 15 months.

B   Two computations: one for the 12 months to 31 December 2021 and the other for the 3 months to 31 March 2022.

C   Two computations: one for the 3 months to 31 March 2021 and the other for the 12 months to 31 March 2022.

D   Two computations: the company can choose the lengths as long as neither is more than 12 months.

Abend Ltd prepared accounts for the year ended 30 September 2021.

The trading profit before capital allowances was £870,000. The company had capital allowances of £25,000 for the year.

The company sold shares at a gain of £57,000 in June 2021 and donated £10,000 of the proceeds to charity.

(b)   **Calculate Abend Ltd's taxable total profits and corporation tax payable for the year ended 30 September 2021, completing the table below. Enter 0 (zero) if an amount is nil and show a deduction as a negative figure.**

	£
Trading income	
Investment income	
Chargeable gains	
Qualifying charitable donations	
Taxable total profits	
Corporation tax payable	

46   LONG LTD AND SHORT LTD

Long Ltd had a period of account of 18 months ended 31 March 2022 and so must apportion income and payments between the accounting periods for tax purposes.

(a)   **Tick the appropriate box for each item to indicate how it will be treated for corporation tax purposes.**

	Time apportion	Separate computation	Period in which it arises
Chargeable gains			
Capital allowances			
Trading profits			
Qualifying charitable donations			

Short Ltd prepared accounts for the six months ended 31 December 2021.

The trading profit after capital allowances was £156,000. The company had bank interest income of £1,000 for the six month period.

A chargeable gain of £20,000 arose on 1 August 2021.

(b)   **Calculate Short Ltd's taxable total profits and corporation tax payable for the period ended 31 December 2021, completing the table below. Enter 0 (zero) if an amount is nil and show a deduction as a negative figure.**

	£
Trading income	
Investment income	
Property income	
Chargeable gains	
Qualifying charitable donations	
Taxable total profits	
Corporation tax payable	

47   SOIR LTD

(a)   **Identify which ONE of the following statements is correct in relation to the calculation of taxable total profits (TTP).**

A   Qualifying charitable donations are deductible from trading profits

B   Dividend income should be excluded from TTP

C   Chargeable gains should be excluded from TTP

D   Capital allowances are deducted from total profits to give TTP

Soir Ltd prepared accounts for the year ended 31 March 2022.

The trading profit before capital allowances was £230,000.

The company had bank interest income of £12,000 receivable for the year ended 31 March 2022. Soir Ltd donated £5,000 of this to charity.

A chargeable gain of £15,000 arose in July 2021.

Soir Ltd had a balancing charge of £6,700 for the year ended 31 March 2022.

(b) **Calculate Soir Ltd's taxable total profits and corporation tax payable for the year ended 31 March 2022, completing the table below. Enter 0 (zero) if an amount is nil and show a deduction as a negative figure.**

	£
Trading income	
Investment income	
Chargeable gains	
Qualifying charitable donations	
Taxable total profits	
Corporation tax payable	

48 COUPE LTD

Coupe Ltd's period of account is the 15 months ended 31 December 2021.

Use the income and payments for the 15 month period given below, to calculate the taxable total profits for each accounting period. Show deductions as negative figures and enter a 0 (zero) in boxes if an amount is nil.

	Total	First accounting period	Second accounting period
	£	£	£
Trading income before capital allowances	15,750		
Capital allowances (£5,000 for the first period, £2,000 for the second period)	7,000		
Trading income after capital allowances			
Rental income (£500 per month)	7,500		
Interest income (£200 per month)	3,000		
Chargeable gain on asset sold on 1 January 2021	800		
Donation to a national charity paid on 31 December 2021	1,000		
Taxable total profits			

49 MERCURY LTD

Mercury Ltd has the following results for the nine months ended 31 March 2022:

	£
Trading profits before capital allowances	250,000
Dividend income	27,000
Bank interest income	1,000
Chargeable gains	13,000
Capital losses b/f	5,000
Qualifying charitable donation	2,000
Balancing charge	5,700

Calculate Mercury Ltd's taxable total profits and corporation tax payable for the nine months ended 31 March 2022, completing the table below. Enter 0 (zero) if an amount is nil and show a deduction as a negative figure.

	£
Trading income	
Investment income	
Chargeable gains	
Qualifying charitable donations	
Taxable total profits	
Corporation tax payable	

50 PANGOLIN LTD

Pangolin Ltd has the following results for the 16 months ended 31 March 2022:

	£
Tax adjusted trading profits before capital allowances	80,000
Rental income	22,000
Chargeable gain on 11 November 2021	61,000
Qualifying charitable donation on 1 July 2021	3,000

The company was entitled to capital allowances of £3,100 in the first accounting period and £1,600 in the second accounting period of this 16 month period of account.

Calculate the taxable total profits and the corporation tax liability of Pangolin Ltd for each accounting period in this 16 month period of account.

	First accounting period	Second accounting period
	£	£
Trading profit		
Property income		
Chargeable gains		
Qualifying charitable donations		
Taxable total profits		
Corporation tax payable		

THE ADMINISTRATIVE REQUIREMENTS FOR UK TAX LAW

Key answer tips

Administrative requirements are important and will be tested in Task 8, which is the longest task in the assessment. This is likely to be a lengthy multi-part task, which could include questions on the rules relating to payments of tax (including the calculation of payments on account and payment dates for companies), filing of returns, penalties, as well as the rules for enquiries, record keeping and notifying chargeability.

The Business Tax reference material provided in your assessment covers these topics in the section headed 'Payment and administration'.

51 IRFAN

(a) **State when the following are due:**

(i) First instalment of income tax for tax year 2021/22:

(ii) Final payment of income tax for tax year 2021/22:

(iii) Capital gains tax payable for tax year 2021/22:

(iv) Second instalment of class 4 NICs for tax year 2021/22:

(b) **Irfan asks whether the following statements are true or false.**

Tick the appropriate box for each statement.

	True	False
An individual must retain tax records for his/her business for 2021/22 until 5 April 2024		
If an individual is seven months late in submitting the tax return for 2021/22, he/she will receive a maximum penalty of £200		
The maximum penalty for a mistake in a tax return due to carelessness is 70%		
If an individual's balancing payment for 2021/22 is two months late he/she can be charged a late payment penalty of 5%		
A company with a period of account ending 30 September 2021 must submit its tax return by 30 September 2022		
Interest is charged on late payments of balancing payments and instalments		

Diamon Ltd began to trade on 1 April 2019. The company submitted its corporation tax return for the year ended 31 March 2020 on 28 February 2021. The augmented profits for that year were £150,000.

HMRC opened an enquiry into this corporation tax return on 15 September 2021. During the enquiry, the directors of Diamon Ltd disclosed an error to HMRC that was deliberately made. The directors had created false documents in relation to the error.

(c) **(i)** **State the date by which Diamon Ltd had to inform HMRC of the start of its first accounting period.**

(ii) **State the due date for payment of Diamon Ltd's corporation tax liability for the year ended 31 March 2020.**

(iii) **State the latest date that HMRC could have opened an enquiry into the return for the year ended 31 March 2020.**

(iv) **The minimum percentage of potential lost revenue that could be charged as a penalty in respect of the error is**

(v) **If Diamon Ltd did not keep proper records for the year ended 31 March 2020, the company is liable to a penalty of**

52   PAYMENTS AND PENALTIES

(a)   Tick the appropriate box for each statement about payments on account (POA).

	True	False
POAs are not required if the income tax and class 4 NIC payable for the previous year by self-assessment is less than £1,000		
POAs for 2021/22 are due on 31 July 2022 and 31 January 2023		
POAs are not required if more than 80% of the income tax and capital gains tax liability for the previous year was met through tax deducted under PAYE		
POAs of class 2 NICs are never required		
POAs of class 4 NICs are optional; the taxpayer can choose to pay under monthly direct debit or quarterly invoice if they prefer		

(b)   State the first payday for corporation tax for a company with augmented profits of £900,000, assuming:

(i)   a six month period ended 31 March 2022:

(ii)   a nine month period ending 31 December 2021:

(iii)   a 12 month period ended 31 January 2022:

(iv)   a seven month period ended 31 October 2021.

(c)   (i)   What is the maximum penalty for submitting a corporation tax return more than six but less than 12 months late?

A   £100

B   £200 plus 10% of the tax due

C   £200

D   £200 plus 20% of the tax due

(ii)   What is the maximum penalty for deliberate understatement without concealment in a tax return?

A   £100

B   10% of tax unpaid

C   70% of tax unpaid

D   100% of tax unpaid

    (ii)   **What is the penalty for a company's failure to keep records for six years?**

        A   Up to £3,000 for each accounting period affected

        B   Up to £6,000 for each accounting period affected

        C   Up to £3,000 in total

        D   Up to £6,000 in total

    (iv)   **What is the penalty for late filing of an income tax return if it is less than three months late?**

        A   £100

        B   £200

        C   £300

        D   10% of tax unpaid

53   NAGINA

(a)   **For each of the following statements, fill in the blanks:**

    (i)   An individual pays the second instalment of income tax under self-assessment for 2021/22 on ....

    (ii)   An individual must file a paper income tax return for 2021/22 by ....

    (iii)   A company with augmented profits of £400,000 for the year ended 31 December 2021 must pay its corporation tax by ....

    (iv)   A .... company pays by instalments based on the .... year's profits

(b)   **Nagina asks whether the following statements are true or false.**

    Tick the appropriate box for each statement.

	True	False
The maximum penalty for a sole trader failing to keep records is £3,000 per accounting period		
The maximum penalty for a failure by an individual to notify chargeability is 100% of the tax due but unpaid		
A late payment penalty can apply to payments on account of income tax		
Companies can choose whether to file paper tax returns or file online		

Jane submitted her 2020/21 tax return on 13 January 2022.

(c)   (i)   **By what date must HMRC give notice if they wish to commence a compliance check?**

        A   31 January 2022

        B   31 January 2023

        C   13 January 2023

        D   30 April 2023

(ii) **Jane asks whether the following statements are true or false.**

Tick the appropriate box for each statement.

	True	False
If Jane fails to produce documents during an enquiry, she may suffer a £300 penalty		
If Jane tells HMRC about a careless error in her 2020/21 return during an enquiry, the penalty can be reduced to nil		
Interest is only payable on a late balancing payment, not late payments on account		
If Jane submits her 2021/22 tax return on 20 January 2023, she will have until 31 January 2024 to make an amendment		

54 MANINDER

A company has prepared its accounts for the year ended 31 March 2022.

(a) **For the following, state when each is due:**

    (i) Submission of the corporation tax return:

    (ii) Payment of corporation tax liability, assuming augmented profits are below £1,500,000:

    (iii) First instalment of corporation tax liability, assuming the company is required to pay by quarterly instalments:

    (iv) Final instalment of corporation tax liability, assuming the company is required to pay by quarterly instalments:

(b) **Maninder asks whether the following statements are true or false.**

Tick the appropriate box for each statement.

	True	False
The filing deadline for electronic submission of an individual's 2021/22 tax return is 31 January 2023		
A self-employed individual is required to keep records to support his/her 2021/22 tax return until 31 January 2028		
There is no penalty for late submission of an individual's tax return as long as it is less than six months late		
If a company makes a mistake in the tax return due to failure to take reasonable care, there is a penalty of up to 30%		
An individual should make the first payment on account for 2021/22 on 31 January 2023		

(c) **Janet asks whether the following statements are true or false.**

Tick the appropriate box for each statement.

	True	False
If an individual is eight months late in submitting the tax return for 2021/22, he/she will receive a penalty of £200		
The maximum penalties for errors made by individuals in their tax returns vary from 20% to 100%		
If a company fails to keep records for the appropriate period of time, it can be fined up to £2,000		
A company with a period of account ending on 30 June 2021, must keep its records until 30 June 2029		
Late payment penalties are not normally imposed on payments on account		

55 LAREDO

(a) **Laredo asks whether the following statements are true or false.**

Tick the appropriate box for each statement.

	True	False
All business tax records for an individual should be kept for at least four years.		
The maximum penalty for not keeping records is £2,000.		
An individual whose income tax and class 4 NICs payable by self-assessment for the previous tax year is less than £1,000 is not required to make payments on account.		
Tax on chargeable gains is paid in two instalments on 31 January in the tax year and 31 July following the end of the tax year.		

Candice is a partner in a trading partnership. Her liabilities to income tax and national insurance contributions (NICs) for recent years are as follows:

	2020/21 £	2021/22 £
Income tax	4,000	6,000
Class 2 NICs	159	159
Class 4 NICs	2,070	2,970

(b) **Calculate the total amount of income tax and class 4 NICs payable on each of the following dates.**

(i) 31 July 2022:

(ii) 31 January 2023:

Calculate the amount of class 2 NICs payable on each of the following dates.

(iii) 31 July 2022:

(iv) 31 January 2023:

Rubi Ltd previously prepared accounts to 31 December each year. The directors decided to change the accounting date to 30 September to better align with their seasonal trade. Recent results are:

	Year ended **31 December 2020**	Period ended **30 September 2021**
	£	£
TTP = augmented profits	1,800,000	1,000,000
Corporation tax payable	342,000	190,000

(c) **In respect of the year ended 31 December 2020:**

(i) the first payment of corporation tax is due by

(ii) the amount payable by that date is

In respect of the period ended 30 September 2021.

(iii) the first payment of corporation tax is due by

(iv) the amount payable by that date is

56 AMIR

Amir worked as an employee until 30 April 2020. He joined a partnership on 1 May 2020.

Amir submitted his tax return for 2020/21 two months late. He paid his income tax liability and national insurance contributions (NICs) for 2020/21 of £3,450 on the same date. Amir had not been required to make payments on account.

(a) **Select from the list below the date by which Amir should have:**

(i) notified HMRC of his chargeability to tax

(ii) submitted his 2020/21 tax return online

(iii) paid his income tax and NIC liabilities for 2020/21

Options:

1 May 2020

5 October 2020

31 January 2021

5 April 2021

5 October 2021

31 January 2022

Calculate the penalties payable by Amir. Enter your answers in whole pounds. Enter 0 (zero) if the amount is nil.

(iv)   Late filing of 2020/21 return

(v)   Late payment of 2020/21 income tax and NIC liabilities

Lamb Ltd is required to make quarterly instalment payments of corporation tax for its year ended 31 December 2021. Instead, the company paid its entire corporation tax liability for the year ended 31 December 2021 on 31 March 2022 in a single payment.

(b)   **Select whether each of the following statements are true or false.**

    Tick the appropriate box for each statement.

	True	False
Lamb Ltd has paid all four quarterly instalment payments late for the year ended 31 December 2021.		
Lamb Ltd pays interest on the late payment of corporation tax.		
Lamb Ltd's augmented profits exceed £1,500,000 for the year ended 31 December 2021.		
Lamb Ltd should have made quarterly instalments based on 25% of the corporation tax liability for the previous year.		

Roger, a sole trader, submitted his 2020/21 tax return on 29 December 2021.

(c)   **Complete the sentences by selecting from the list of dates below.**

(i)   Roger may amend his 2020/21 tax return at any point until _____

(ii)   Roger must pay his first payment on account of income tax for 2021/22 by _____

(iii)   Roger must pay his class 2 national insurance contributions for 2021/22 by _____

(iv)   Roger must keep records in respect of his 2020/21 tax return until _____

Options

31 January 2022

31 July 2022

29 December 2022

31 January 2023

31 January 2026

5 April 2026

31 January 2027

57   SHEP LTD

Shep Ltd submitted its corporation tax return for 31 March 2020 on 30 October 2021. On the same date it paid its corporation tax liability of £76,000 in full.

Shep is not a large company for quarterly instalment purposes.

(a)   Complete the following sentences in respect of the year ended 31 March 2020

(i)   The corporation tax payment due date was

(i)   The corporation tax return filing due date was

Calculate the following penalty amounts arising due to the late filing of the tax return

(iii)   The total fixed rate penalty

(iv)   The tax-geared penalty

(b)   For each of the following scenarios, select the appropriate penalty from the following list.

Options

£0

£10

£60

£100

£300

£3,000

15% of potential lost revenue

30% of potential lost revenue

50% of potential lost revenue

70% of potential lost revenue

100% of potential lost revenue

(i)   Sophia has received interest from a loan she made to her brother. She thought this was not taxable as it was a private arrangement and so did not include it on her 2019/20 tax return. Her accountant has told her it is taxable and Sophia has disclosed the error to HMRC. The minimum penalty is

(ii)   In its corporation tax return for the year ended 30 June 2020, Ash Ltd understated its property income by £12,000 due to a data entry error by the financial controller. The income is usually the same each year. The financial controller disclosed the error during an HMRC enquiry. The minimum penalty is

(iii)   Jed, a sole trader, failed to keep proper records for 2018/19. He may be liability to a penalty of

[   ]

(iv)   HMRC are conducting an enquiry into Sandra's income tax return for 2019/20. An initial penalty for failure to provide documents to HMRC has been issued. Sandra may also incur a daily penalty of

[   ]

(v)   The finance director of Noirt Ltd deliberately recorded expenditure on factory repairs as £160,000 when the invoice showed an amount of £60,000. The corporation tax return for the year ended 30 September 2020 was submitted using the finance director's figures, and she amended the invoice to show the inflated amount. She makes no disclosure to HMRC. The maximum penalty is

[   ]

(c)   Select whether each of the following statements are true or false.

Tick the appropriate box for each statement.

	True	False
Janine does not submit her income tax return earlier than the due date as doing so would give HMRC longer to raise an enquiry into the return.		
A company which is not large pays its corporation tax 11 months after the end of the accounting period. The company will be charged a penalty of 5%.		
A large company pays quarterly instalments based on an estimate of the corporation tax liability for that period.		
The maximum penalty for late filing of an income tax return is 100% of the tax due.		

TAX PLANNING AND THE RESPONSIBILITIES OF THE BUSINESS AND AGENT

Key answer tips

Tax planning and ethical issues relating to the agent's responsibilities to HMRC are important areas and will be tested in Task 9 of the assessment. This will be a human marked written style task which may have many parts. The task could include using the badges of trade to identify whether a client is trading. Tax planning questions may involve understanding the tax implications of different business structures and extraction of profits. A tax planning question may focus on opportunities for spouses and civil partners.

To answer tax planning questions you need to understand the tax rates which apply to individuals and companies. The Business Tax reference material provided in your assessment gives these rates in the sections headed 'Income tax', 'National Insurance (NI)' and 'Corporation Tax'.

Questions on ethical matters may involve tax planning, tax avoidance and tax evasion, and the reporting and confidentiality issues surrounding these.

58   LEANNE

Leanne is the sole director and shareholder of a company. Leanne takes a salary of £30,000 from the company each year.

Leanne sets the level of dividend she takes from the company so that it falls within the remainder of her basic rate band and she avoids paying income tax at the higher rate.

Your firm acts for several clients including Leanne who are sole directors and shareholders of their own companies.

(a)   (i)   **Explain whether Leanne's action to limit the dividend is tax planning, tax avoidance or tax evasion.**

(ii)   **Identify whether you can share information about Leanne with HMRC and other clients in these circumstances.**

Your manager has forwarded the following email to you from Melanie. Melanie is an investment banker and a client of your firm.

'I inherited a number of items of furniture following the death of my father. I renovated the furniture, kept some of the items and sold the rest for a total of £4,000. I know that the items of furniture are exempt for the purposes of capital gains tax, but I am not sure of my position in relation to income tax. Also, I enjoyed the renovation work so much that I am considering purchasing more furniture, which I will then restore and sell at a profit.'

(b)   **In relation to the badges of trade, explain whether you think Melanie will be treated as carrying on a trade.**

Ahmed operates his business through a company. He is the sole shareholder and director. The company makes annual trading profit of around £30,000, after Ahmed pays himself a salary of £10,000. Ahmed's only other income is dividend income from quoted investments of £8,000 per annum.

Ahmed wants to take as much further profit from the company as possible and wants to know the tax implications of paying this as a dividend or a further salary.

(c)   **Explain the tax implications of Ahmed taking as much profit as he can as dividends or paying himself as much additional salary as he can.**

59   STUART

Stuart runs his business as a sole trader. He purchased plant for £10,000 but when claiming the annual investment allowance recorded this as £100,000 to increase the allowance available.

(a)   (i)   **Explain the difference between tax evasion and tax avoidance.**

(ii)   **Identify whether Stuart's action is tax evasion or tax avoidance.**

Stuart's accountant Clara is an AAT member. She must follow the principle of confidentiality.

(b)   **Identify the circumstances when Clara would disclose information about a client to another party.**

Clara has responsibilities to her employer, the AAT, Stuart and HMRC.

(c)   **Identify to whom Clara owes the greatest duty of care.**

Misha has previously been an employee but now wants to start her own business.

Misha expects she will make profits around £12,000 in the first year. She will take out as much profit from the business as possible in the first year as she has no other income. She wants to grow the business to make annual profits of £50,000 within the next two years, and then she will not extract all the profits each year.

(d)   **Explain the tax implications of Misha operating her business as a sole trader and alternatively, through a company.**

60   SAKI AND IAN

You work at a firm of accountants. Saki and her husband Ian are both clients of the firm. Ian telephones you and asks for a copy of Saki's last tax return. They need it to prove Saki's level of income when taking out a bank loan.

(a)   (i)   **Identify a step your firm must take before giving Saki's tax return to Ian, explaining why the action is necessary.**

(ii)   **Explain whether your answer would be different if the bank had approached you for Saki's tax return directly.**

Judith and Charmaine are in a civil partnership together. Judith operates a business through a company with no employees. Charmaine is a part-time artist. Charmaine's annual trading profits are £5,000 and she has no other income.

Judith takes a mix of salaries and dividends from the company such that her income is £60,000. Judith also has interest income from building society deposits of £2,000 per annum.

Charmaine understands finance and technology better than Judith and occasionally helps Judith with the company's accounts and with computer issues. Charmaine has suggested the company could pay her £400 per month as a part-time employee for this work.

(b) **Explain tax planning opportunities for Judith and Charmaine to reduce their overall tax liabilities and whether the company taking on Charmaine as an employee would achieve this.**

Oli and Tamar are unconnected but operate businesses in the same sector, each making annual profits of £60,000. Oli is a sole trader. Tamar trades through a company. Both are bidding for a new contract worth profit of £40,000 per year from a new client. The successful bidder will retain the profits of this new contract in their business for future investment.

(c) **Explain the differences in how the profits of the new contract would be taxed in each case.**

61 FRED

Fred is a lawyer. He bought a painting in 2014 for £40,000 and displayed it in his home. In 2021 he decided to sell the painting to raise funds towards buying a new house. He made repairs to the frame and listed the painting for sale in a specialist art magazine. The painting was sold for £50,000.

(a) **Explain whether Fred is likely to be treated as carrying on a trade, referring to the badges of trade.**

You work for a firm of accountants. Jessica is a sole trader and one of the firm's clients. She has contacted you to say that a friend has introduced her to a company which has promised to save her income tax if she takes part in a scheme operated by the company. The scheme is legal but relies on a loophole in the law.

The company operating the scheme has contacted you directly for details of Jessica's trading profits for the last tax year.

(b) (i) **Define tax planning, tax avoidance and tax evasion.**

(ii) **Identify whether Jessica would be involved in tax planning, tax avoidance or tax evasion if she participates in the scheme.**

(iii) **Explain the action you should take in response to the approach from the company operating the scheme.**

Motsi is the sole shareholder and director of her company. Motsi's only income is from the company. Motsi usually takes a salary of £10,000 and a dividend of around £45,000 to extract the entire profits of the company each year. She will continue to do this. However, the company has recently won a new contract which generates a further profit of £15,000.

Motsi wants to know how much of the additional £15,000 profit she could extract either as dividend or salary.

(c) **Explain the tax implications of Motsi taking dividend or salary to extract the additional profits of £15,000.**

62   NINA

Nina is a new AAT student at the accountancy firm where you work. She tells you that she had told her friend about the tax affairs of one of your former high-profile clients. She says she knows she does not have to worry about confidentiality as she is not yet an AAT member and, in any case, the client has now left the firm.

(a)   **Explain why Nina is wrong in her actions and statements about confidentiality.**

While preparing a client's tax return, you discover he has engaged in tax evasion by omitting income from his previous tax return. He refuses to disclose this to HMRC.

(b)   **Explain how the principle of confidentiality affects whether you should disclose this to any regulatory authorities.**

Franz regularly buys items in charity shops and then sells them soon after on online auction sites for a higher price. He has purchased a labelling machine to speed up the packaging process. He estimates that each week he has a cash profit of £250 from the sales.

(c)   **With reference to the badges of trade, explain whether Franz is likely to be treated as carrying on a trade.**

Tia is a wealthy individual with property income of £160,000 and dividend income from investments of £50,000 per annum.

She has started a small business selling her own art work online. She expects to make trading profits of £20,000 per annum from this venture, while maintaining the level of her other income. She will use the money made after tax to pay for a family holiday each year.

Tia has not yet decided whether to set up a company or trade as an unincorporated trader.

(d)   **Advise Tia of the tax advantages and disadvantages of using a company or operating as a sole trader. Calculations are not required.**

63   NASHEEN

Nasheen is a student member of the AAT. The accountancy firm where she works acts for Pamela and Mick, a married couple. Mick is ill and a colleague has suggested you discuss Mick's tax affairs with his wife so that his tax return is not delayed.

Nasheen is concerned as she thinks she must follow the rules of confidentiality irrespective of the situation.

(a)   (i)   **State the condition which must be met for Nasheen to be able to discuss Mick's tax affairs with Pamela.**

(ii)   **Identify occasions when the rules of confidentiality are overridden for an accountant.**

Anton is the sole shareholder and director of a company. His only income is from the company.

The company makes trading profits of £100,000 for the year.

Anton wants to understand the rates of tax on:

–   the profits of the company

–   the income paid to him, if he extracts the maximum amount as dividends

–   the income paid to him, if he extracts the maximum amount as salary.

(b)   (i)   **Explain the rates of tax charged on the profits of the company, dividends paid by the company and salary paid by the company.**

        (ii)   **Explain the different taxes and rates of tax which would apply if Anton had instead operated the business as a sole trader.**

64   VICKY

Vicky is a sole trader who prepares her accounts to 5 April each year.

For the year ended 5 April 2022 she recorded trading profits of £49,900 in her 2021/22 tax return. This does not include a large sale completed in March 2022 which gave a profit of £10,000. Instead she recorded this sale in her accounts as taking place on 20 April 2022 to avoid paying higher rate tax in 2021/22.

Vicky tells you that this is just a timing difference, so she does not think this is a problem.

(a)   **Explain whether Vicky's delayed recording of the sale is tax planning, tax evasion or tax avoidance.**

You discover that a client has engaged in tax evasion by failing to report the gain on the sale of an item of plant.

(b)   **State your responsibilities in relation to reporting the tax evasion.**

Jason bought an old car from a scrap yard two years ago and spent his weekends working on repairs to make it roadworthy. He had intended to use the car himself but a friend offered to buy it and Jason accepted. Jason enjoyed the repair work and so used the proceeds to buy another car to repair.

Now each month Jason buys an old car and then repairs it prior to selling it at a profit. He has rented a lock up garage to carry out this work. He uses the money he receives from selling a car to buy the next one.

(c)   **With reference to the badges of trade, explain whether Jason is likely to be treated as carrying on a trade.**

Marion and Geoff are married. Geoff is retired and has no income.

Marion is a sole trader with trading profits of £70,000 per annum.

Marion inherited shares in quoted companies from her sister. She receives dividend income of £20,000 per annum from the shares.

(d)   **Identify and explain an opportunity for the couple to minimise their overall income tax liability. Your answer should also consider any possible long-term tax implications of this tax planning.**

TRADING LOSSES

Key answer tips

Task 10 of the assessment will cover losses for sole traders, partnerships and companies and will be partly human marked. It may be computational, written but with reference to figures given, theory based or a combination. It is important that you understand the difference between the rules applicable to individuals compared with companies. It is possible that both could be tested in one task – so you must be clear as to which set of rules you are applying.

The Business Tax reference material provided in your assessment covers losses in the sections headed 'Trading losses'.

65 NICHOLAS

Nicholas, a junior member of the tax department, asks whether the following statements about losses are true or false.

(a) **Tick the appropriate box for each statement.**

	True	False
A trading loss made by a company can only be offset against trading profits from the same trade when carrying the loss back		
The amount of a trading loss offset against current year profits of a company can be set to preserve the deduction for qualifying charitable donations		

Luka is a sole trader who prepared accounts to 31 March each year.

On 31 March 2022, Luka ceased to trade as his business had made a loss for the year of £80,000. He then started a job with annual employment income of £30,000.

Previously the business had been profitable:

Year ended 31 March	Trading profits
	£
2018	50,000
2019	40,000
2020	35,000
2021	20,000

Luka has savings income of £10,000 in each tax year.

(b) **Explain the loss relief options for Luka, indicating the rates at which income tax would be saved for each option. Recommend the best option for Luka. Full calculations of income tax savings are not required.**

66   JOANNA

(a)   **Identify which one of the following statements made by Joanna is correct.**

A   A loss made by a sole trader must be relieved against total income in the current tax year.

B   For a loss made by a sole trader to be relieved in the current tax year, it must first have been relieved in the preceding tax year.

C   A loss made by a sole trader can only be relieved against profits of the same trade when carried forward to future years.

D   A loss made by a sole trader can be relieved against total income arising in future years.

Cheny Ltd has traded for many years. The company had previously made profits but in the year ended 31 December 2021 invested heavily in new production methods which were not successful. The company made a trading loss of £590,000 that year and ceased to trade on 31 December 2021.

Trading profits for recent years were:

Year ended 31 December	Trading profits
	£
2017	400,000
2018	200,000
2019	270,000
2020	160,000

Cheny Ltd had interest income of £10,000 each year. The company made charitable donations of £20,000 each year.

In January 2019, the company sold a building giving rise to a chargeable gain of £80,000.

(b)   **Explain the optimum loss relief for Cheny Ltd.**

67   STILTON LTD

Stilton Ltd has the following results for the two years ended 31 December 2021 and predicted results for the year ended 31 December 2022.

Year ended 31 December	2020	2021	2022
	£	£	£
Trading profits/(loss)	8,000	(40,000)	1,000
Bank interest	1,000	600	600
Chargeable gain	1,200	Nil	500
Qualifying charitable donation	150	150	150

Stilton Ltd wishes to use its trading loss as soon as possible.

(a)   **Explain the use of Stilton Ltd's trading loss.**

Cheddar Ltd had a loss for the year ended 30 June 2022, but continued to trade.

(b)   What is the earliest accounting period in which the company could offset the loss?

A   Year ended 30 June 2021

B   Year ended 30 June 2020

C   Year ended 30 June 2019

D   Year ended 30 June 2018

68   KANE

(a)   **Kane asks whether the following statements are true or false.**

Tick the appropriate box for each statement.

	True	False
A sole trader can offset a trading loss against total income in the current and/or the previous tax year, in any order		
For a trading loss made by a company to be relieved in the preceding accounting period, it must first have been relieved in the current accounting period		
Use of trading loss relief by a company can result in wasted qualifying charitable donations		

Samantha has traded for many years profitably. However, due to the liquidation of a major client Samantha's profits first decreased and then she made a trading loss of £38,000 for the year ended 5 April 2022.

The trading profits of the business in previous years were:

Year ended 5 April	Trading profits
	£
2019	28,000
2020	30,000
2021	16,000

Samantha has met with some prospective clients and hopes she will be able to make trading profits of £25,000 in the year ended 5 April 2023. She has also had to take a part-time job with employment income of £20,000 per annum from 2022/23.

Samantha has property income of £15,000 each year.

She wants to claim loss relief as early as possible.

(b)   (i)   **Explain how Samantha's trading loss would be used to achieve relief as soon as possible, and the potential income tax savings. Detailed calculations of tax savings are not required.**

(ii)   **Identify how the loss could be used if instead of claiming loss relief as early as possible, Samantha's objective is to save the most tax. Explain any disadvantages with this option. Detailed calculations of tax savings are not required.**

69 GREEN LTD

Green Ltd has the following results for the year ended 31 March 2022:

	£
Trading profits	175,000
Interest income	30,000
Net chargeable gains	20,000
Qualifying charitable donation	10,000

The company had trading losses brought forward from the previous period of £230,000.

Green Ltd takes advantage of all beneficial claims that can be made.

(a) **Identify the loss relief in the year ended 31 March 2022. Explain any unrelieved amounts at 31 March 2022 and how these amounts may be used in future.**

(b) **Tick the appropriate box for each statement.**

	True	False
A sole trader cannot restrict the amount of loss offset in the current year to preserve the personal allowance		
A sole trader can carry forward a loss for a maximum of four years		

(c) **Identify the differences between carry forward loss relief of trading losses in a company and by a sole trader.**

70 JOYCE, LIZ AND RON

(a) **Tick the appropriate box for each statement.**

	True	False
A trading loss made by a company can only be offset against trading profits from the same trade when carrying the loss forward		
The trading loss of a company in the period it ceases to trade can be carried back three years after current year relief		

Joyce, Liz and Ron were in partnership during the year ended 31 March 2022.

Joyce has been a partner for many years and will continue to be. She has savings income of £20,000 each year.

Liz has been a partner for many years but retired from the partnership on 31 March 2022. She has property income of £13,000 each year.

Ron joined the partnership on 1 April 2021. Prior to this Ron had been on a career break for a year to look after his children. He had earned employment income before this of £30,000 per year until and including 2019/20.

In recent years, the main product of the partnership was falsely claimed to be harmful to the environment. Profits declined and the partnership had a trading loss of £54,000 in the year ended 31 March 2022. Sales have now recovered and a trading profit of £40,000 is expected in the year ended 31 March 2023.

The trading profits in recent years were:

Year ended 31 March	Trading profits
	£
2018	62,000
2019	50,000
2020	30,000
2021	24,000

Partnership profits are always shared equally been partners.

(b) **Explain the loss relief options for each partner. You should discuss the possible tax savings under each option although actual calculations of savings are not required. Recommend the best option for each partner.**

71 DONAL

Donal worked as a solicitor earning employment income of £200,000 until leaving his job on 5 April 2020. From 6 April 2020 he has lectured a law school part-time earning £60,000 per annum.

On 6 April 2021 he also set up his own business writing and publishing legal teaching material. In his first year of trade ended 5 April 2022, he made a loss of £45,000. However, he expects to make trading profits of £25,000 in 2022/23.

Donal has no other income.

(a) **Explain the loss relief options for Donal. Recommend the best option for Donal. Full calculations of income tax savings are not required but your answer should be relevant to the amounts in the scenario.**

Brick Ltd has been trading since 1 October 2017, usually making a profit. The company invested large amounts in new plant and machinery during the year ended 30 September 2020 and so made a trading loss after claiming capital allowances.

Trading results of the company were:

Year ended 30 September	Trading profits/(loss)
	£
2018	150,000
2019	200,000
2020	(400,000)
2021	100,000

Brick Ltd had property income of £24,000 in each year since the commencement of trade. In June 2021, Brick Ltd sold an item of machinery for a gain of £56,000.

The company makes qualifying charitable donations of £15,000 each year.

Brick Ltd wants to claim loss relief as early as possible.

(b) **Explain how Brick Ltd's trading loss is used.**

BUSINESS DISPOSALS

Key answer tips

This section covers the tax implications of business disposals by an individual. You may be required to calculate the gains, capital gains tax, or the post-tax proceeds on such disposals in Task 11 of the assessment.

Reliefs covered are business asset disposal relief and gift relief.

The Business Tax reference material provided in your assessment covers these topics in the sections headed 'Capital gains tax' and 'Chargeable gains reliefs'. Note that rollover relief is not tested in this task for individuals – it is only tested for companies as seen earlier in this exam kit.

72 SUSAN AND RACHEL

Susan made a chargeable gain of £550,000 on the sale of her business. She had owned the business for ten years and is now retiring. She is a higher rate taxpayer.

She also realised a gain of £15,000 on the sale of an antique table.

(a) **Identify which of the following statements is NOT correct.**

A The taxable gain on the antique table will be taxed at 20%

B Business asset disposal relief is available on the business gain as all of the conditions have been satisfied

C The chargeable gain on the business, after the deduction of the annual exempt amount, will be taxed at 10%

D The annual exempt amount is deducted from the gain on the antique table, leaving all of the business gain to be taxed

Rachel sold her sole trader business on 31 March 2022 for £400,000. The proceeds were allocated to the assets of the business as follows:

Asset	Proceeds	Cost
	£	£
Workshop	200,000	115,000
Plant	15,000	70,000
Inventory	10,000	8,000
Goodwill	175,000	0

(b) Calculate the capital gain or loss on the disposal of each asset. Enter 0 (zero) if there is no gain or loss. Enter a loss as a negative amount.

Asset	Capital gain/(loss)
	£
Workshop	
Plant	
Inventory	
Goodwill	

(c) Select whether each of the following statements about gift relief is true or false.

Tick the appropriate box for each statement.

	True	False
Gift relief is available on a gain on the gift of shares in a quoted investment company provided the donor owned at least 5% of the shares		
The gain on a gift of any holding of shares in an unquoted trading company qualifies for gift relief		
Gift relief defers the gain on a gift of a qualifying asset until the recipient sells the asset		
A gain on the gift of an asset used in the trade of the donor does not qualify for gift relief if the donor has not owned the asset for at least two years		

73 NORMAN

Norman has owned 15% of the shares in a trading company since May 2000. He is an employee of the company.

He sells all his shares in December 2021, making a gain before reliefs of £700,000. He has made no other disposals and is a higher rate taxpayer.

(a) Calculate Norman's capital gains tax payable for 2021/22.

```
┌──────────────────────────────┐
│                              │
└──────────────────────────────┘
```

(b) State the deadline for claiming business asset disposal relief for a disposal in 2021/22.

Choose from one of the following options:

31 January 2022;   31 January 2023;   31 January 2024;   31 January 2025;
31 October 2022;   31 October 2023;   31 October 2024;   31 October 2025

Bharat sold his sole trader business on 1 July 2021.

Bharat had nil tax written down value for capital allowances at the start of the period in which he ceased to trade. He made no purchases during the period.

The proceeds given for his assets, and their original costs, are shown below:

Asset	Proceeds	Cost
	£	£
Storage garage	40,000	25,000
Computer equipment	3,000	10,000
Inventory	16,000	10,000
Goodwill	41,000	0

(c) **For each asset, select one option from the list which describes the tax result of the disposal.**

Choose from one of the following options. You can use each option more than once.

capital gain; capital loss; trading profit increase; trading profit decrease

Asset	Tax effect
Storage garage	
Computer equipment	
Inventory	
Goodwill	

Dinah started her own manufacturing company in January 2012, subscribing £10,000 for 100 shares. She is the sole shareholder.

She has worked for the company since incorporation. On 30 September 2021 she sold her entire shareholding to a competitor for £2,300,000. Dinah paid a solicitor £2,300 in legal fees relating to the sale.

She made no other disposal. Dinah is a higher rate taxpayer.

(d) (i) **Calculate Dinah's taxable gain for 2021/22.**

(ii) **Calculate Dinah's capital gains tax payable for 2021/22.**

(iii) **Calculate Dinah's net proceeds after tax from the sale.**

74   HARRY AND BRIONY

Harry made a gain qualifying for business asset disposal relief of £300,000 in 2020/21.

A further qualifying gain of £5,500,000 was made in 2021/22.

There were no other disposals in either year and Harry is a higher rate taxpayer.

(a)   Calculate Harry's capital gains tax payable for 2021/22.

> [   ]

(b)   Which of the following statements is correct?

A   Gift relief is only available to companies

B   Gift relief is available to both companies and individuals

C   Gift relief is only available to individuals

Briony had operated her sole trader business from 1 July 2006. She sold the business on 1 November 2021 for £790,000. The capital gains allocated to the business assets are as follows:

Asset	Gains
	£
Office building	125,000
Office furniture	0
Goodwill	260,000

Briony is an additional rate taxpayer and has made no other disposals. She makes all beneficial claims.

(c)   (i)   Calculate Briony's taxable gain for 2021/22.

> [   ]

(ii)   Calculate Briony's capital gains tax payable for 2021/22.

> [   ]

(iii)   Calculate Briony's post tax proceeds tax from the sale.

> [   ]

Ranj started to trade on 1 January 2020. He sold his business during 2021/22 and claimed business asset disposal relief.

(d)   (i)   State the earliest date Ranj could have sold his business to qualify for business asset disposal relief.

> [   ]

(ii)   State the date by which Ranj must make the claim for business asset disposal relief.

> [   ]

75   CHERYL

(a)   Identify which one of the following statements is correct.

A   Business asset disposal relief is available on qualifying business gains of up to £1,000,000 for the lifetime of the taxpayer.

B   Business asset disposal relief is restricted to £1,000,000 of gains for each disposal of qualifying business assets.

C   Business asset disposal relief is available for individuals and companies.

D   Business asset disposal relief is available on the sale of individual business assets.

Gio disposes of his sole trader business.

(b)   Select whether each of the following statements about the disposal is true or false.

Tick the appropriate box for each statement.

	True	False
If the tax written down value on the general pool exceeds the disposal value of plant, a balancing allowance arises		
The sale of goodwill which has been generated by Gio may give rise to a capital loss		
If Gio had traded for 13 months, business asset disposal relief would not be available		
An allowable capital loss may arise on the sale of the plant used in the business		

Aljaz bought 2,000 shares in an unquoted trading company on 1 December 2014 for £60,000. This represented a 20% shareholding. On the same day he started work for the company as a sales director.

On 1 February 2022, he gave the shares to his son when their market value was £350,000.

Aljaz has previously made one disposal when he sold a business in January 2012 for £950,000 and claimed business asset disposal relief. He has taxable income of £80,000 in 2021/22.

(c)   (i)   Calculate the gift relief on the share disposal if a gift relief claim is made.

(ii)   Calculate Aljaz's taxable gain for 2021/22 if gift relief is not claimed.

(iii)   Calculate Aljaz's capital gains tax payable for 2021/22 if business asset disposal relief is claimed instead of gift relief.

76   RALF

Ralf operated a sole trader business preparing accounts to 5 April each year. He sold the business on 19 October 2021.

The tax written down value on Ralf's general pool for capital allowances at 6 April 2021 was £5,000 and Ralf made no purchases during the period. He made no disposals until he sold the business.

The sales proceeds for Ralf's assets, and their original costs, are shown below:

Asset	Proceeds	Cost
	£	£
Goodwill	50,000	0
Warehouse	430,000	500,000
Machinery	0	50,000
Inventory	0	15,000

(a)   For each asset, select one option from the list which describes the tax result of the disposal.

Choose from one of the following options. You can use each option more than once.

capital gain; capital loss; trading profit increase; trading profit decrease

Asset	Tax effect
Goodwill	
Warehouse	
Machinery	
Inventory	

Taylor started a trading company on 1 July 2013. She subscribed £1,000 for 1,000 shares. She is the sole shareholder and director. Taylor sold her entire shareholding on 31 December 2021 for £410,000.

Taylor has previously sold a sole trader business in January 2019 making a gain of £2,400,000. She is an additional rate taxpayer and always makes any beneficial tax claims.

(b)   (i)   Calculate Taylor's taxable gain for 2021/22.

(ii)   Calculate Taylor's capital gains tax payable for 2021/22.

(iii)   Calculate Taylor's net proceeds after tax from the sale.

(c)   Select whether each of the following statements about capital gains tax reliefs is true or false.

Tick the appropriate box for each statement.

	True	False
Gift relief is available on a gain on the gift of unquoted trading company shares, regardless of the size of the shareholding		
If a sole trader sells a building but continues to trade, business asset disposal relief is not available		
Business asset disposal relief applies automatically on a disposal of a business if the gain does not exceed £1,000,000		
Business asset disposal relief defers a gain on disposal of unquoted trading company shares until the recipient sells the shares		

77   STEPHAN

Stephan ran a business as a sole trader for eight years. He gave the business to his daughter on 1 March 2022.

The market values of the assets held by the business at 1 March 2022, and their original costs, are as follows:

Asset	Proceeds	Cost
	£	£
Goodwill	80,000	0
Industrial building	870,000	550,000
Plant	20,000	30,000
Inventory	100,000	80,000

(a)   Calculate the capital gain or loss on the disposal of each asset. Enter 0 (zero) if there is no gain or loss. Enter a loss as a negative amount.

Asset	Capital gain/(loss)
	£
Goodwill	
Industrial building	
Plant	
Inventory	

Sajid sold his business on 31 August 2021 after trading for ten years. The proceeds received for his business assets, and the resulting gains and losses are as follows:

Asset	Proceeds	Gain/(loss)
	£	£
Goodwill	100,000	100,000
Factory	600,000	(30,000)
Plant	50,000	0
Inventory	20,000	0

Sajid has taxable income of £30,000 for 2021/22 and has made no other disposals. He makes all beneficial claims.

(b) **(i)** **Calculate Sajid's taxable gain for 2021/22.**

(ii) **Calculate Sajid's capital gains tax payable for 2021/22.**

(iii) **Calculate Sajid's post tax proceeds tax from the sale.**

(c) **Select whether each of the following statements about capital gains tax reliefs is true or false.**

Tick the appropriate box for each statement.

	True	False
If a sole trader gifts an asset used in the trade but continues to trade, gift relief is not available		
Business asset disposal relief reduces the rate of capital gains tax on the gain on the sale of a business		
To qualify for business asset disposal relief on the sale of a business, the trader must have operated the business for at least two years		
There is a lifetime limit of £1,000,000 on gains qualifying for gift relief		

78   LEIGH

Leigh started trading in 2006. He sold his business for £150,000 on 1 November 2021.

The sales proceeds were allocated between the business assets as follows:

Asset	Proceeds	Cost
	£	£
Goodwill	50,000	0
Storage unit	80,000	25,000
Plant	20,000	50,000

(a)   **Calculate the capital gain or loss on the disposal of each asset. Enter 0 (zero) if there is no gain or loss. Enter a loss as a negative amount.**

Asset	Capital gain/(loss)
	£
Goodwill	
Storage unit	
Plant	

(b)   **Select whether each of the following statements about capital gains tax reliefs is true or false.**

Tick the appropriate box for each statement.

	True	False
A trader who ceases to trade after two years, and sells the assets of the business for a gain within four years of the cessation can claim business asset disposal relief		
To claim gift relief on the disposal of unquoted trading company shares, the donor must have worked for the company for two years		
Gift relief is available if quoted trading company shares are gifted, provided the donor had a shareholding of at least 5%		
If the proceeds on the sale of a business exceed £1,000,000, business asset disposal relief is always only partially available		

(c)   **For each of the following disposals, select one option from the list which describes the capital gains tax relief(s) available on the disposal.**

Choose from one of the following options. You can use each option more than once.

business asset disposal relief

gift relief

business asset disposal relief and gift relief

neither business asset disposal relief nor gift relief

Disposal	Capital gains tax relief(s)
Gift of a building used in the continuing trade of a sole trader	
Sale of shares in an unquoted investment company, wholly owned by the seller, where the seller has worked for 20 years	
Gift of a sole trader business which has operated for ten years	
Gift of shares in a quoted trading company where the donor has held 6% of the shares for five years but did not work for the company	
Sale of an interest in a partnership by a partner who joined five years earlier	

Section 2

ANSWERS TO PRACTICE QUESTIONS

ADJUSTING ACCOUNTING PROFITS AND LOSSES FOR TAX PURPOSES

Key answer tips

The chief assessor has commented in the past that when learners have failed in this type of task, it seems to be due to lack of robust knowledge on areas such as lease payments, adjustments for private use by the owner of the business and what is capital expenditure and what is not. A common error would be to adjust for the business use element of the expenses as opposed to adjusting for the private element.

1 GILES

(a)

	Revenue	Capital
Decorating an office	✓	
Computer for a salesman		✓
Office building extension		✓
Electricity for the quarter to 31 March 2022	✓	
Meal to entertain a customer from Germany	✓	
Fork lift truck for the warehouse		✓

(b)

	Allowable	Disallowable	CAs available
Water rates	✓		
Building insurance	✓		
Replacement of factory machinery		✓	✓
Replacement of a severely damaged roof on an office building	✓		
Insurance for motor cars	✓		
Parking fine incurred by an employee	✓		

Tutorial note

1   *Replacement of the whole of an asset such as the factory machinery is a capital item. The replacement of part of an asset, such as the damaged roof of the office building will be treated as revenue expenditure.*

2   *Parking fines incurred by non-senior employees whilst on business activity are allowable for tax purposes.*

2   PHILIP

(a)

	Revenue	Capital
Printer for the office computer		✓
Water rates	✓	
Legal fees for purchase of a building		✓

Tutorial note

Costs relating to the purchase of a capital asset will be included as part of its capital cost. Hence the legal fees incurred on purchase of the building should be debited to capital not revenue expenses. For tax purposes legal fees related to a capital acquisition are always treated as capital expenditure and disallowed in the computation of adjusted profits.

(b)

	Allowable	Disallowable	CAs available
Painting an office	✓		
Car for a salesman		✓	✓
Office building extension		✓	
Gas for the quarter to 30 June 2022	✓		
Van for deliveries		✓	✓
Meal to entertain staff	✓		
Printer for the office computer		✓	✓
Dividends payable		✓	
Costs of a fraud carried out by a director. These costs are not covered by insurance.		✓	

Tutorial note

There are no plant and machinery capital allowances available on office buildings, although the structures and buildings allowance would apply.

Staff gifts and staff entertaining are allowable.

Dividends are appropriations of profit and not allowable as an expense.

The costs of a fraud carried out by directors are not allowable. If the fraud had been carried out by an employee the costs would have been allowed.

3 BROWN

(a)

	Revenue	Capital
Repairs to a boiler	✓	
Insurance for motor cars	✓	
Replacement of a severely damaged roof on a newly-purchased warehouse before being able to use the building		✓
Parking fine incurred by Brown	✓	

Tutorial note

1   Expenditure to repair a newly acquired asset is normally treated as revenue expenditure if the asset is in a serviceable condition when purchased.

However, where the asset cannot be used in the business unless further expenditure is incurred on it, and the purchase price reflects the state of disrepair, any subsequent repair expenditure is treated as part of the original capital cost of purchase of the asset.

2   The parking fine of the owner is a revenue expense and will be deducted in the statement of profit or loss of the business.

It is not a tax allowable expense; however this question does not require you to consider that aspect.

(b) **Tax adjusted trading profit computation – year ended 31 March 2022**

	£
Accounting profit	34,890
Depreciation	2,345
Motor expenses (£4,788 × 50% × 50%)	1,197
Staff Christmas party	0
Gift aid donation	34
Wages to Armadillo's wife (£19,000 – £14,500)	4,500
Capital allowances	(3,460)
Taxable profit	39,506

Tutorial note

1   *50% of the motor expenses relates to Armadillo. Of that 50%, only 50% are allowable as he uses his car 50% for private purposes.*

2   *Entertaining staff is allowable for the business, irrespective of the amount spent.*

3   *The gift aid donation is not allowable in the adjustment of profits computation. Tax relief is available for the donation in Armadillo's personal income tax computation. The operation of this relief is covered in personal tax.*

4   *Salaries paid to family members are allowable provided they represent reasonable remuneration for the services provided to the business. As Armadillo's wife is paid more than the normal salary for the role she performs, the excess is not allowable.*

4   FINN

Tax adjusted trading profit computation – year ended 31 March 2022

	£
Accounting profit	107,270
Wages and salaries	0
Rent and rates	0
Repairs	10,000
Advertising and entertaining	1,050
Accountancy and legal costs	0
Motor expenses (50% × £6,000)	3,000
Leasing costs (15% × £8,000)	1,200
Telephone and office costs	0
Depreciation	26,525
Other expenses (£500 + £400)	900
	42,675
Capital allowances	(21,070)
Taxable profit	128,875

Tutorial note

1   *Gifts to customers costing less than £50 per person per year and carrying a conspicuous advertisement for the business are tax allowable. However, gifts of food, drink, tobacco and vouchers are not allowable.*

2   *15% of the leasing costs for high emission cars (CO_2 emissions over 50g/km) are disallowed.*

3   *The donation to Children in Need is a donation to a national charity and is not allowable in the adjustment of profits computation. Provided the donation is made under the gift aid rules, tax relief is available for the donation in Finn's personal income tax computation. The operation of this relief is covered in personal tax.*

5   JAMIE

Tax adjusted trading profit computation – year ended 31 March 2022

	£
Accounting loss	(22,066)
Jamie's salary	28,000
Sue's salary	12,500
Lisa's salary	0
Rent, rates and insurance	0
Delivery van expenses	0
Salesman's car expenses	0
Jamie's motorbike (30% × £2,250)	675
Depreciation	40,355
Entertaining customers	625
Entertaining staff	0
Recipe books	0
Cost of staff training	0
Caviar (2 × £150)	300
	82,455
Capital allowances	(42,236)
Taxable profit	18,153

Tutorial note

1   Salaries paid to family members are allowable provided they represent reasonable remuneration for the services provided to the business. As Jamie's wife does not work for the business at all, none of that expense is allowable. It is assumed, however, that the salary paid to his daughter for her role as Financial Controller of the business is reasonable remuneration.

2   Entertaining staff is allowable for the business, irrespective of the amount spent. Any other form of entertaining is not allowable.

3   Gifts to customers costing less than £50 per person per year and carrying a conspicuous advertisement for the business are tax allowable. Therefore the recipe book expenditure will be allowable.

4   Where the owner takes goods out of the business, for tax purposes, it is treated as a sale to himself at full market value. Jamie must therefore account for the profit element of the transaction (£200 – £50 = £150 per tin of caviar) in his adjustment of profit computation.

6   REBECCA

Tax adjusted trading profit computation – year ended 31 March 2022

	£
Accounting profit	79,164
Profit on sale of equipment	(1,280)
Accountancy fees	0
Payroll fees	0
Increase in specific impaired debt provision	0
Increase in general impaired debt provision	268
Trade debts written off	0
Trade debts recovered	0
Repairs and maintenance	0
Depreciation	7,424
Heating	0
Rent, rates and insurance	3,000
Van expenses	0
Car expenses	2,690
Wages and salaries	18,000
Telephone and office costs	0
Diaries	0
Parking fines	280
Capital allowances	(11,642)
Taxable profit	97,904

Tutorial note

1   *If a sole trader makes a general provision in the accounts, it is not allowable for tax purposes, but specific provisions are allowable.*

2   *Gifts to customers costing less than £50 per person per year and carrying a conspicuous advertisement for the business are tax allowable. Therefore the cost of the diaries will be allowable.*

3   *Parking fines incurred by the owner are not allowable, even if they are incurred whilst on business activity.*

7   BENABI

Tax adjusted trading profit computation – year ended 31 March 2022

	£
Accounting profit	33,489
Wages and salaries – Benabi's salary	6,000
Rent, rates and insurance	0
Repairs to plant	0
Advertising and entertaining – boxes of chocolates	1,250
Accountancy and legal costs	0
Motor expenses – Benabi's motor expenses	1,100
Depreciation	8,001
Telephone and office costs	0
Other expenses – subscription to gym	220
Capital allowances	(9,955)
Taxable profit	40,105

Tutorial note

1   *Salaries paid to family members are allowable provided they represent reasonable remuneration for the services provided to the business. It is assumed that £8,000 is reasonable remuneration for Benabi's wife working in the marketing department.*

2   *Gifts to customers costing less than £50 per person per year and carrying a conspicuous advertisement for the business are tax allowable. However, gifts of food, drink, tobacco and vouchers are not allowable.*

3   *Entertaining staff is allowable for the business, irrespective of the amount spent.*

4   *Personal expenses, such as the subscription to the gym for the owner, are not allowable.*

8 FRANKLIN LTD

(a)

	Allowable	Disallowable
Advertising costs incurred in January 2021	✓	
Entertaining prospective customers in February 2021		✓
Dividends paid to shareholders on 2 January 2022		✓

Tutorial note

Pre-trading expenditure is allowable if it is incurred in the seven years before trade commences and is expenditure that would be allowable if trade had commenced. The advertising is allowable but the entertaining would not be allowable if trade had started so is not allowable if incurred before trade starts.

Dividends are appropriations of profit and not allowable as an expense.

(b)

	Silvain	Alice	Lucille	Pascal
Should use the trading allowance	✓		✓	
Given automatically	✓			
Elect to receive			✓	
Elect not to receive		✓		
Taxable trading income (£)	0	0	2,750	3,220

Tutorial note

Silvain has trading income below £1,000, so will automatically receive the trading allowance and will have not have to declare any trading income for the tax year 2021/22.

Alice will also automatically receive the trading allowance, but should elect to be treated on the normal basis, as she has an allowable loss, which is available for tax relief.

Lucille has trading income in excess of £1,000, so will not receive the trading allowance automatically. However, as her expenses are less than £1,000 she should elect to receive the trading allowance instead of deducting her expenses.

Pascal will also be taxed on the normal basis automatically and should not elect for a different treatment as his expenses exceed £1,000.

	Alice	Lucille	Pascal
	£	£	£
Trading income	690	3,750	6,300
Less: Expenses	(740)		(3,080)
Trading allowance		(1,000)	
Trading profit / (loss to carry forward)	(50)	2,750	3,220

CAPITAL ALLOWANCES

Key answer tips

In previous assessments, the biggest area of confusion has been the handling of cars. Remember that their treatment depends on the CO_2 emissions and whether they are used privately by the owner of the business – you must know the WDA available in each case and which column they should be included in. Always consider whether private use needs to be adjusted for – remember no adjustment is ever required for private use in a company, nor for the private use of an employee in a sole trader's business.

Other areas of difficulty are long periods of account for a company (which must be split into two separate periods) and the handling of capital allowances when a business ceases trading (remember no AIA, WDA or FYA should be given, simply a balancing adjustment in each column).

9   BROAD LTD

(a)   **Capital allowances computation – year ended 31 December 2021**

	FYA	AIA	Super deduction	General pool	Special rate pool	Allowances
	£	£	£	£	£	£
TWDV b/f				140,000	26,000	
Additions:						
Plant		10,000				
Machinery			1,020,000			
FD's car	34,000					
Sales director's car				32,000		
FYA	(34,000)					34,000
AIA		(10,000)				10,000
Super deduction			(1,020,000)			1,326,000
Disposals: (lower of cost and SP)				(10,000)	(13,800)	
				162,000	12,200	
WDA (18%/6%)				(29,160)	(732)	29,892
TWDV c/f				132,840	11,468	
Total allowances						1,399,892

Tutorial note

1   *The plant purchased in March 2021 qualifies for the annual investment allowance (AIA).*

2   *The machinery purchased in May/June 2021 qualifies for the super deduction at 130% because it is new plant purchased by a company on or after 1 April 2021.*

3   *Private use of assets by an employee is irrelevant in a company's capital allowances computation; the allowances are available in full. The individual is assessed on the private use element in his/her personal income tax computation as an employment benefit.*

4   *Capital allowances on car purchases are calculated based on the CO_2 emissions of the car as follows:*

   –   *new car with zero CO_2 emissions:*

        eligible for a FYA of 100% (i.e. Finance Director's car)

   –   *CO_2 emissions of between 1 – 50g/km:*

        put in main pool and eligible for a WDA at 18% (i.e. Sales Director's car)

   –   *CO_2 emissions of > 50g/km:*

        put in special rate pool – eligible for a WDA at 6%.

5   *Disposals are deducted at the lower of cost and sale proceeds. The deduction for the machinery is therefore restricted to £10,000.*

(b)   (i)   The amount of expenditure which qualifies for structures and buildings allowance is £280,000.

      (ii)   The structures and buildings allowance is £2,800 (£280,000 × 3% × 4/12).

Tutorial note

The structures and buildings allowance (SBA) is available on the construction of a new building but also on the purchase from a developer of a new building which has not yet been used.

Costs relating to the land do not qualify for SBA. The purchase of the office furniture qualifies for plant and machinery capital allowances.

The SBA is available from when the building is first brought into use i.e. 1 December 2021.

10   WELL LTD

(a)   **Capital allowances computation – year ended 31 March 2022**

	Super deduction	General pool	Special rate pool	Allowances
	£	£	£	£
TWDV b/f		134,500	36,000	
Additions:				
Machinery	644,167			
Finance Director's car		34,500		
Super deduction	(644,167)			837,417
Disposals: (Lower of cost and SP)		(10,000)	(11,800)	
		159,000	24,200	
WDA				
18%		(28,620)		28,620
6%			(1,452)	1,452
TWDV c/f		130,380	22,748	
Total allowances				867,489

Tutorial note

1   *The machinery purchased in May 2021 qualifies for the super deduction because it is new plant purchased by a company on or after 1 April 2021.*

2   *Private use of assets is irrelevant in a company's capital allowances computation; the allowances are available in full. The individual is assessed on the private use element in their personal income tax computation as an employment benefit.*

3   *Capital allowances on car purchases are calculated based on the CO_2 emissions of the car. As the Finance Director's new car has CO_2 emissions of between 1 – 50g/km, it is put in the main pool and is eligible for a WDA at 18%.*

The Finance Director's original car had CO_2 emissions such that it had been included in the special rate pool.

4   *Disposals are deducted at the lower of cost and sale proceeds.*

(b)   The zero emission car costing £20,000 qualifies for 100% first year allowance and this is not time apportioned for the long period.

The TWDV on the general pool gives rise to a WDA of 18% × 15/12, time apportioned due to the long period.

Tutorial note

First year allowances are not increased or decreased due to long or short periods.

The WDA on the general pool or special rate pool is increased/decreased for a long/short period.

11   PINKER LTD

(a)   **Capital allowances computation – five months ended 31 May 2021**

	FYA	AIA	General pool	Special rate pool	Allowances
	£	£	£	£	£
TWDV b/f			345,980	23,000	
Additions:					
Plant		539,000			
Car			18,000		
Zero emission car	13,790				
FYA (100%)	(13,790)				13,790
AIA (£1,000,000 × 5/12)		(416,667)			416,667
		———	122,333		
			486,313	23,000	
WDA (18% × 5/12)			(36,473)		36,473
WDA (6% × 5/12)				(575)	575
TWDV c/f			449,840	22,425	
			———	———	
Total allowances					467,505
					———

Tutorial note

1   *This computation is for the five-month period ending 31 May 2021. Therefore you must remember to time apportion the AIA and WDAs available by 5/12, but not the FYA.*

2   *Capital allowances on car purchases are calculated based on the CO_2 emissions. Cars with CO_2 emissions of between 1 – 50g/km are put in the main pool and are eligible for a WDA at 18% per annum.*

Cars with zero CO_2 emissions are eligible for a FYA of 100%.

(b)   **Structure and buildings allowance**

	True	False
The allowance for a year is 3% of the brought forward tax written down value of the building		✓
The allowance is time apportioned if the building was brought into use part way through the year	✓	
Expenditure on land does not qualify for the allowance	✓	
If the building is sold to a second user, the allowance for the second user is 3% of the price paid by the second user		✓
The allowance is available to both companies and unincorporated businesses	✓	

Tutorial note

The structures and buildings allowance is 3% of the original qualifying expenditure on the building. This is either the construction cost, or the price paid to the developer if the building has not yet been used. The allowance is not calculated on the TWDV.

Unlike the WDA, the allowance is time apportioned if the building is only brought into use part way through a period or is sold part the way through the period.

A subsequent purchaser claims allowances on the same original expenditure, not on the price it pays for the building.

12 SARAH

Capital allowances computation – year ended 31 December 2021

	AIA	FYA	General pool	Private use asset	Allowances
	£	£	£	£	£
TWDV b/f			65,100	14,500	
Additions:					
Zero emission car		20,000			
FYA (100%)		(20,000)			20,000
Furniture	11,000				
Van	8,600				
Plant	15,500				
	———				
	35,100				
AIA	(35,100)				35,100
	———		0		
Disposals: (lower of cost and SP)			(14,200)	(10,000)	
			———	———	
			50,900	4,500	
Balancing allowance				(4,500) × 80%	3,600
WDA (18%)			(9,162)		9,162
			———	———	
TWDV c/f			41,738	0	
			———	———	———
Total allowances					67,862
					———

Tutorial note

1   *Private use of assets by the owner is relevant and allowances must be restricted to the business use proportion only.*

2   *Capital allowances on car purchases are calculated based on the CO_2 emissions.*

New cars with zero CO_2 emissions are eligible for a FYA of 100%.

3   *CO_2 emissions are irrelevant for vans. Vans are eligible for the AIA and any balance goes into the general pool.*

4   *Remember that the super deduction is not available for unincorporated businesses, but the annual investment allowance is available.*

(b)   The answer is D.

Tutorial note

The costs of obtaining planning permission do not qualify for the structures and buildings allowance (SBA).

The rate is 3% per annum. The rate of 6% relates to the WDA for the special rate pool.

A subsequent purchaser can claim allowances, but based on the original construction expenditure (or cost of purchase from the developer), and not on the price the subsequent purchaser pays for the building.

(c)   The answer is B.

Tutorial note

The maximum AIA available is £1,000,000 regardless of when the plant is purchased. It is only time apportioned for a short period of account, not if the plant is purchased part way through the period.

The super deduction is available because the plant is purchased new, by a company, on or after 1 April 2021.

The writing down allowance is only time apportioned for a short period of account, not if the plant is purchased part way through the period.

A first year allowance of 100% is available for new zero emission cars.

13   DAVE AND NICK

(a)   (i)   **Capital allowances computation – eight months ended 31 August 2021**

	AIA	General pool	Private use asset 1 (Dave's car B.U. 70%)	Private use asset 2 (Nick's car B.U. 60%)	Allowances
	£	£	£	£	£
Additions:					
Plant	7,680				
Furniture	12,450				
	20,130				
Cars			15,300	10,200	
AIA	(20,130)				20,130
		0			
WDA (6% × 8/12)			(612) × 70%		428
WDA (18% × 8/12)				(1,224) × 60%	734
TWDV c/f		0	14,688	8,976	
Total allowances					21,292

Tutorial note

1   *The partnership commenced on 1 January 2021 and the first accounts are prepared to 31 August 2021. This computation is therefore for an eight-month period. Remember to time apportion the WDAs available by 8/12. The AIA is also time apportioned but the maximum amount of £666,667 (£1,000,000 × 8/12) exceeds the purchases in the period.*

2   *Capital allowances on car purchases are calculated based on the CO_2 emissions of the car as follows:*

– *new car with zero CO_2 emissions:*

eligible for a FYA of 100% (i.e. none in this question)

– *CO_2 emissions of between 1 – 50g/km:*

eligible for a WDA at 18% (i.e. Nick's car)

– *CO_2 emissions of > 50g/km:*

eligible for a WDA at 6% (i.e. Dave's car).

3   *Remember to calculate the allowance in full on the private use cars and then adjust for private use (i.e. only claim the business proportion of the allowance).*

(ii)   **Capital allowances computation – seven months ended 31 March 2022**

	General pool	Private use asset 1 (Dave's car B.U. 70%)	Private use asset 2 (Nick's car B.U. 60%)	Allowances
	£	£	£	£
TWDV b/f	0	14,688	8,976	
Plant	10,000			
	10,000			
Disposal	(22,000)			
Disposal – MV		(12,500)	(7,500)	
	(12,000)	2,188	1,476	
Balancing charge	12,000			(12,000)
Balancing allowances		(2,188)	(1,476)	
		× 70%		1,532
			× 60%	886
Net balancing charge				(9,582)

Tutorial note

When a business ceases to trade there is no AIA or WDA in the final accounting period. Additions are added to the relevant columns. Proceeds are compared to the TWDV of each column and balancing charges or allowances calculated.

Remember that only the business proportion of balancing allowances/balancing charges can be claimed/charged where they relate to assets with private use by an owner of the business.

(b)

	True	False
The super deduction is available on the purchase of plant and buildings on or after 1 April 2021 by a company		✓

Tutorial note

The super deduction is only available on the purchase of new plant, not buildings. It is only available for companies on purchases on or after 1 April 2021.

14   PIRBRIGHT LTD

(a)   Capital allowances computation – year ended 30 June 2021

	FYA	AIA	Super deduction	General pool	Special rate pool	Allowances
	£	£	£	£	£	£
TWDV b/f				81,000	28,900	
Additions:						
Machinery		640,000				
Equipment			50,000			
Low emission car	21,000					
Car – SRP					38,600	
FYA (100%)	(21,000)					21,000
AIA (max £1,000,000)		(640,000)				640,000
Super deduction (130%)			(50,000)			65,000
		———				
				0		
Disposals (lower of cost and SP)				(11,250)	(15,400)	
				———	———	
				69,750	52,100	
WDA						
18%				(12,555)		12,555
6%					(3,126)	3,126
				———	———	
TWDV c/f				57,195	48,974	
				———	———	———
Total allowances						741,681
						———

Tutorial note

1   *The machinery purchased before 1 April 2021 does not qualify for the super deduction but the annual investment allowance is available. For the new equipment purchased after 1 April 2021, the super deduction gives a greater allowance.*

2   *Private use of assets is irrelevant in a company's capital allowances computation; the allowances are available in full. The individual is assessed on the private use element in his/her personal income tax computation as an employment benefit.*

3   *Capital allowances on car purchases are calculated based on the CO_2 emissions of the car. A car with CO_2 emissions in excess of 50g/km is put into the special rate pool and is eligible for a WDA.*

   New cars with zero emission are eligible for a FYA of 100%.

(b)   The plant qualifies for the annual investment allowance of 100%. The limit of the AIA is £250,000 (£1,000,000 × 3/12). The remainder of the expenditure of £50,000 qualifies for WDA of 18%, time apportioned 3/12.

Tutorial note

The maximum AIA and WDA must be decreased for a short period.

The super deduction is not available to unincorporated businesses.

---

15   AMOLI

(a)   Capital allowances computation – 15 months ended 31 March 2022

	AIA	FYA	General pool	Private use asset	Allowances
	£	£	£	£	£
TWDV b/f			23,400	8,700	
New electric car		30,000			
FYA (100%)		(30,000) × 70%			21,000
Machinery	15,000				
Van	25,000				
	————				
	40,000				
AIA	(40,000)				40,000
	————		0		
Employee car			20,000		
Disposals (lower of cost and SP)			(12,000)	(11,000)	
			————	————	
			31,400	(2,300)	
Balancing charge				2,300 × 70%	(1,610)
				————	
WDA (18% × 15/12)			(7,065)		7,065
			————		
TWDV c/f			24,335		
			————		————
Total allowances					66,455
					————

Tutorial note

1   *Capital allowances on car purchases are calculated based on the CO_2 emissions.*

New cars with zero CO_2 emissions are eligible for a FYA of 100%. This is not time apportioned for the long period.

2   *Private use of assets by the owner is relevant and allowances including the FYA must be restricted to the business use proportion only. This also applies on disposal in relation to the balancing charge.*

3   *CO_2 emissions are irrelevant for vans. Vans are eligible for the AIA and any balance goes into the general pool.*

4   *Remember that the super deduction is not available for unincorporated businesses, but the annual investment allowance is available.*

5   *Disposals are deducted at the lower of cost and sales proceeds. The deduction for the packaging equipment is therefore restricted to £12,000.*

6   *The WDA is increased due to the length of the period.*

(b)   The answer is C.

Tutorial note

The structures and buildings allowance is 3% for the year, but the building was only brought into use part way through the year. The allowance is time apportioned for six months from 1 July 2021.

The furniture is new expenditure incurred by a company on or after 1 April 2021 and so the super deduction (130%) applies such that the maximum allowance is £97,500.

The construction costs qualify for the structures and buildings allowance, but the planning permission costs and the land costs do not.

(c)   **Explanation of treatment of disposals**

The disposal proceeds are deducted as these are less than cost.

Car A has been used privately by Liam. A balancing charge arises as the disposal value of £6,000 exceeds the TWDV of £5,000. Only the business use element of the difference is included as the balancing charge i.e. 70% × £1,000.

Private use by an employee does not restrict allowances and so car B is not treated separately. The disposal proceeds for car B are deducted from the general pool, but no balancing adjustment arises as Liam is still trading. WDA is calculated on the balance as normal.

Tutorial note

A disposal of a car which qualified for 100% FYA is deducted from the general pool.

A balancing allowance only arises in the general pool if the trader ceases to trade.

A balancing adjustment arises on a private use asset as this is not included in the pool.

The private use adjustment applies to balancing adjustments, just as it applies to WDA.

BASIS PERIOD RULES

Key answer tips

When applying the basis of assessment rules be careful to start with the correct tax year, as otherwise this will have a knock on effect on the rest of your answer. You must also carefully count months, as any mistakes with this simple task will cost you marks. It is recommended that you work your answers on paper first – checking the dates and months, and ensuring that the dates seem logical. Remember that a taxpayer will always be taxed on twelve months' worth of profits, except in the first and last tax year of the business.

16 KURT

(a) B

(b) A

(c) C

(d) B

(e) £25,800

Working

Tax year	Basis period	Assessment £
2018/19	1 October 2018 – 5 April 2019 (6/9 × £22,500)	15,000
2019/20	1 October 2018 – 30 September 2019 £22,500 + (3/12 × £43,200)	33,300
2020/21	Current year basis year ended 30 June 2020	43,200
Overlap profits	1 October 2018 – 5 April 2019 (6/9 × £22,500)	15,000
	1 July 2019 – 30 September 2019 (3/12 × £43,200)	10,800
		25,800

(f)

	True	False
If Kurt had chosen an accounting date of 31 December rather than 30 June, his overlap profits would have been greater		✓

Tutorial note

An April accounting date has the highest number of months of overlap profits and a March accounting date has none. Therefore as the date moves from April to March the months of overlap profit decrease. The June accounting date leads to nine months of overlap profit but the December date would have three months overlap.

17   ROBERT

(a)   (i)   B

(ii)   C

(iii)   B

(iv)   £17,100

Working

Tax year	Basis period	Assessment
		£
2019/20	1 January 2020 – 5 April 2020 (3/10 × £32,000)	9,600
2020/21	1 January 2020 – 31 December 2020 £32,000 + (2/12 × £45,000)	39,500
2021/22	Current year basis year ended 31 October 2021	45,000

Overlap profits	1 Jan 2020 – 5 Apr 2020	(3/10 × £32,000)	9,600
	1 Nov 2020 – 31 Dec 2020	(2/12 × £45,000)	7,500
			17,100

(b)

	True	False
Cerys' basis period for 2021/22 is the 15 month period from 1 July 2020 to 30 September 2021	✓	
Cerys' assessable profits for 2021/22 will be increased by the overlap profits of £3,000		✓

Tutorial note

The overlap profits will reduce Cerys' assessable trading profits for 2021/22.

---

18   JAVID

(a)   (i)   B

(ii)   A

(iii)   C

(iv)   C

Working

Tax year	Basis period	Assessment
		£
2020/21	1 January 2021 – 5 April 2021 (3/17 × £34,000)	6,000
2021/22	6 April 2021 – 5 April 2022 (12/17 × £34,000)	24,000
2022/23	1 June 2021 – 31 May 2022 (12/17 × £34,000)	24,000
Overlap profits	1 June 2021 – 5 Apr 2022 (10/17 × £34,000)	20,000

Tutorial note

The first tax year is the year in which the business commenced trading, i.e. 2020/21, therefore the second tax year is 2021/22. The opening year rules dictate that when a business does not have a year end falling inside of a tax year (2021/22) then the profits will be taxed on an actual basis (i.e. 6 April – 5 April).

(b)

	True	False
An accounting date of 31 March means no overlap profits arise	✓	
An accounting date of 31 March maximises the delay between generating profits and being taxed on those profits		✓

Tutorial note

The accounting date of 31 March is best for reducing overlap profits – there are none – but minimises the time between generating profits and paying the tax.

An accounting date of 30 April would give the greatest delay between generating profits and paying tax, but would also give rise to the most overlap profits (11 months).

19 CHARIS

(a) B

(b) The profits in her second year of trading (2021/22) are £18,000

(c) The profits in her third year of trading (2022/23) are £24,000

(d) Her overlap profits are £1,500

Working

Tax year	Basis period	Assessment
		£
2020/21	1 January 2021 – 5 April 2021	
	(3/14 × £21,000)	4,500
2021/22	1 March 2021 – 28 February 2022	
	(12/14 × £21,000)	18,000
2022/23	Current year basis	
	Year ended 28 February 2023	24,000
Overlap profits	1 March 2021 – 5 April 2021	
	(1/14 × £21,000)	1,500

Tutorial note

Where the period of account ending in the second tax year is more than 12 months then the basis period is the 12 months to the accounting date ending in the second tax year, i.e. 12 months to 28 February 2022.

(e)

	True	False
If Charis had chosen an accounting date of March instead of February, overlap profits would be nil.	✓	
When Charis ceases to trade, the overlap profits will increase her taxable profits in the last year of trade.		✓

Tutorial note

The overlap profits reduce the taxable profits in the last year of trade.

20 GORDON

(a) C

(b) A

(c) B

Working

Tax year	Basis period	Assessment £
2020/21	Penultimate year of assessment Current year basis Year ended 30 June 2020	132,000
2021/22	Final period of assessment 1 July 2020 – 30 November 2021 Year ended 30 June 2021 5 months ended 30 November 2021	120,000 56,000
		176,000
	Less: Overlap profits	(22,000)
		154,000

(d) His overlap profits remaining after cessation are £0.

(e)

	True	False
His overlap profits from commencement would have been lower	✓	
The total profits taxed over the lifetime of the business would have been lower		✓

Tutorial note

The accounting date of 30 September leads to lower overlap profits on commencement of trade.

The overall profits taxed – the total profits of the business – are the same over the course of a business, regardless of the accounting date chosen.

21   **HENRIETTA**

(a)   C

(b)   C

(c)   A

(d)   B

(e)   £4,913

(f)   B

Working

Tax year	Basis period	Assessment £
2019/20	1 February 2020 – 5 April 2020 (2/16 × £7,860)	983
2020/21	6 April 2020 – 5 April 2021 (12/16 × £7,860)	5,895
2021/22	12 months ended 31 May 2021 (12/16 × £7,860)	5,895
Overlap profits	1 June 2020 – 5 April 2021 (10/16 × £7,860)	4,913

Tutorial note

There is no set of accounts ending in the second tax year, 2020/21, so the assessment is based on the profits in the tax year 6 April 2020 – 5 April 2021.

If Henrietta had chosen an accounting date of 31 August (I.e. later in the tax year), then the overlap profits would be lower.

22   MELISSA

(a)   (i)   2022/23

(ii)   £12,000

(iii)   £3,000

Working

Tax year	Basis period	Assessment £
2021/22	Penultimate year of assessment Current year basis Year ended 30 September 2021	12,000
2022/23	Final period of assessment 1 October 2021 – 30 June 2022 Less: Overlap profits	5,000 (2,000)
		3,000

(b)

	True	False
Jimmy's first year of trade is 2021/22.		✓
If Jimmy prepares his first set of accounts for the year ended 28 February 2022, he will have overlap profits of 1/12 of his first year's profits.	✓	
If Jimmy wishes to delay the payment of tax on his profits for as long as possible, he should choose an accounting date of 30 April.	✓	

Tutorial note

The starting date of trade, 1 March 2021, falls in the tax year 2020/21.

An accounting date of 30 April delays payment of tax, but also gives rise to the highest overlap profits.

ANALYSING PROFITS AND LOSSES OF A PARTNERSHIP AND CALCULATING NICS

Key answer tips

The allocation of assessable profits between partners is another area of difficulty that the chief assessor has highlighted in the past.

Calculating the NICs payable by partners causes learners the most difficulty. Remember that it may be necessary to apportion partnership profits before calculating the class 4 NICs and that each partner will be liable to their own class 2 NICs.

23 SUE, WILL AND TERRI

(a) **Allocation of profit**

	Sue	Will	Terri	Total
	£	£	£	£
Period to 31 March 2021				
Profit share	25,200	16,800	0	42,000
Period to 30 September 2021				
Profit share	16,800	16,800	8,400	42,000
Total	42,000	33,600	8,400	84,000

Workings

Period to 31 March 2021

The profit to be allocated is £84,000 × 6/12 = £42,000 which is then split 3:2

Period to 30 September 2021 is £84,000 × 6/12 = £42,000 which is then split 2:2:1

(b) **Class 4 NICs payable**

	£
(£50,270 − £9,568) = £40,702 × 9%	3,663.18
(£85,000 − £50,270) = £34,730 × 2%	694.60
	——————
	4,357.78
	——————

(c) **Class 2 NICs payable**

	£
(£3.05 × 52 weeks)	158.60
	———

Tutorial note

Self-employed taxpayers pay class 4 NICs based on their taxable trading profits in excess of £9,568 and the fixed rate class 2 NICs of £3.05 per week provided taxable trading profits exceed £6,515. The level of drawings is irrelevant.

24 JENNY AND HARVEY

(a) **Allocation of profit**

	Jenny	Harvey	Total
	£	£	£
Period to 31 March 2021			
Salary	0	0	0
Profit share	18,750	18,750	37,500
Total for period	18,750	18,750	37,500
Period to 31 December 2021			
Salary	30,000	0	30,000
Profit share	41,250	41,250	82,500
Total for period	71,250	41,250	112,500
Total for year	90,000	60,000	150,000

Workings

Period to 31 March 2021

The profit to be allocated is £150,000 × 3/12 = £37,500 which is then split 1:1 as there is no salary in the first period.

Period to 31 December 2021

The profit to be allocated is £150,000 × 9/12 = £112,500

Salary to Jenny is £40,000 × 9/12 = £30,000

Remaining profit is (£112,500 − £30,000) = £82,500 which is then split 1:1

Tutorial note

In the period to 31 December 2021 a salary is paid which must be dealt with before allocating profits using the profit share. The first step is to find the profit for the period as usual (here, £112,500 being nine months of the total profit). The salary is then allocated. The remaining profit is calculated (after salary) of £82,500 and this is then apportioned according to the profit sharing ratio.

(b) (i) **Amount chargeable to class 4 NICs at 9%**

(£50,270 – £9,568)   £40,702
                                                        ─────────

(ii) **Amount chargeable to class 4 NICs at 2%**

(£100,000 – £50,270)   £49,730
                                                        ─────────

(iii) **Class 2 NICs payable**

                                                            £
(£3.05 × 52 weeks)   158.60
                                                        ─────────

Tutorial note

Class 1 primary NICs are paid by employees on their salary. Self-employed individuals pay class 4 NICs on their profits.

25 SALLY, BARRY, BILL AND BEA

(a) **Allocation of profit**

	Sally	Barry	Bill	Bea	Total
	£	£	£	£	£
Period to 31 August 2020					
Interest on capital	1,000	1,250	2,500	1,125	5,875
Profit share	81,389	40,695	40,694	20,347	183,125
Total for period	82,389	41,945	43,194	21,472	189,000
Period to 31 May 2021					
Interest on capital	0	0	0	0	0
Profit share	206,182	154,636	103,091	103,091	567,000
Total for period	206,182	154,636	103,091	103,091	567,000
Total	288,571	196,581	146,285	124,563	756,000

Workings

Period to 31 August 2020

The profit to be allocated is £756,000 × 3/12 = £189,000

Interest on capital is £80,000/£100,000/£200,000/£90,000 × 5% × 3/12 giving total of £5,875.

Remaining profit is (£189,000 – £5,875) = £183,125 which is then split 4:2:2:1

Period to 31 May 2021

The profit to be allocated is £756,000 × 9/12 = £567,000 which is then split 4:3:2:2 as there is no interest in the second period

(b) **Class 2 NICs payable**

	£
(£3.05 × 52 weeks)	158.60

(c) **Class 4 NICs payable**

	£
(£41,000 – £9,568) = £31,432 × 9%	2,828.88

Tutorial note

Self-employed taxpayers pay class 4 NICs based on their taxable trading profits in excess of £9,568 and the fixed rate class 2 NICs of £3.05 per week provided taxable trading profits exceed £6,515.

---

26   ALVIN, SIMON AND THEODORE

(a)   **Allocation of profit**

	Alvin	Simon	Theodore	Total
	£	£	£	£
Period to 31 July 2021				
Profit share	13,200	7,920	5,280	26,400
Period to 31 January 2022				
Profit share	13,200	13,200	0	26,400
Total	26,400	21,120	5,280	52,800

Workings

Period to 31 July 2021

The profit to be allocated is £52,800 × 6/12 = £26,400 which is then split in the ratio 5:3:2

Period to 31 January 2022

The profit to be allocated is £52,800 × 6/12 = £26,400 which is then split 1:1

(b) **Amount liable to class 4 NICs at 9%**

Thomas is older than state pension age   £0

(c) **Class 4 NICs**

£

(£35,000 – £9,568) = £25,432 × 9%   2,288.88

Tutorial note

Self-employed taxpayers pay class 4 NICs based on their taxable trading profits in excess of £9,568 and the fixed rate class 2 NICs of £3.05 per week provided taxable trading profits exceed £6,515.

However, if the taxpayer has reached state pension age by the start of the tax year there is no class 4 liability.

---

27 SIAN AND ELLIE

(a) (i) **Allocation of profit**

	Sian	Ellie	Owen	Total
	£	£	£	£
Period to 30 April 2021				
Profit share	18,000	9,000	0	27,000
Period to 31 July 2021				
Profit share	4,500	3,000	1,500	9,000
Total for y/e 31 July 2021	22,500	12,000	1,500	36,000
Total for y/e 31 July 2022	30,000	20,000	10,000	60,000

Workings

Period to 30 April 2021

The profit to be allocated is £36,000 × 9/12 = £27,000 which is then split 2:1.

Period to 31 July 2021 is £36,000 × 3/12 = £9,000 which is then split 3:2:1.

Year ended 31 July 2022

The profit of £60,000 is split in the ratio 3:2:1

(ii)   **Owen: assessable profits**

2021/22

	£
Profits from 1 May 2021 to 5 April 2022 (11 months)	
Period to 31 July 2021 (3 months)	1,500
8/12 of y/e 31 July 2022 (£10,000 × 8/12)	6,667
	8,167

2022/23

y/e 31 July 2022	10,000

Tutorial note

Partnership tax adjusted trading profits must be allocated between partners using the profit sharing arrangements of the accounting period. Once this is done the basis period rules can be applied to the profit shares of each partner to determine the taxable profits for the tax year.

Owen has just joined the partnership so opening year rules will apply to him as if he were a sole trader commencing on 1 May 2021 and preparing accounts to 31 July each year.

(b)   (i)   **Class 4 NICs payable by Amelie**

	£
Share of partnership profits	
(£75,000 − £5,000) × 60%	42,000
(£42,000 − £9,568) = £32,432 × 9%	2,918.88

(ii)   **Class 4 NICs payable by Alexander**

	£
Share of partnership profits	
£5,000 + ((£75,000 − £5,000) × 40%)	33,000
(£33,000 − £9,568) = £23,432 × 9%	2,108.88

(iii)   **Class 2 NICs payable by Amelie**

	£
(£3.05 × 52 weeks)	158.60

Tutorial note

When calculating NICs for partners you must first apportion the partnership profits between the partners following the normal partnership rules. You should then apply the normal NIC rules to those apportioned profits, not the partnership 'salary'.

Class 2 NICs are payable by all partners in full.

28 NOEL, DAVID AND LUCY

(a) **Allocation of profit**

	Noel	David	Lucy	Total
	£	£	£	£
Period to 31 December 2021				
Salary	0	0	0	0
Loss share	(10,000)	(30,000)	(20,000)	(60,000)
Period to 31 March 2022				
Salary	0	4,000	0	4,000
Loss share	(12,000)	(12,000)	0	(24,000)
Total for the year	(22,000)	(38,000)	(20,000)	(80,000)

Workings

Period to 31 December 2021

The loss to be allocated is £80,000 × 9/12 = £60,000 which is then split 1:3:2 as salaries are not paid in this period.

Period to 31 March 2022

The loss to be allocated is £80,000 × 3/12 = £20,000.

Salary is allocated to David of £16,000 × 3/12 = £4,000.

The remaining loss to share in the profit sharing ratio is therefore £24,000 (£20,000 + £4,000). The salary means a greater loss must be split to compensate. This is then split in the ratio 1:1

(b) (i) **Class 4 NICs payable at 9%**

(£50,270 – £9,568) = £40,702 × 9%   £3,663.18

(ii) **Class 4 NICs payable at 2%**

(£70,000 – £50,270) = £19,730 × 2%   £394.60

(iii) **Total class 4 NICs payable**

£3,663.18 + £394.60   £4,057.78

(c) £0

Tutorial note

Self-employed taxpayers pay class 4 NICs based on their taxable trading profits in excess of £9,568 and the fixed rate class 2 NICs of £3.05 per week provided taxable trading profits exceed £6,515.

29 TOMMY, GRACE AND BRIDIE

(a) **Allocation of profit**

	Tommy	Grace	Bridie	Total
	£	£	£	£
Period to 30 September 2021				
Salary	0	0	0	0
Profit share	80,000	20,000	0	100,000
Period to 31 March 2022				
Salary	10,000	10,000	0	20,000
Profit share	40,000	20,000	20,000	80,000
Total for y/e 31 March 2022	130,000	50,000	20,000	200,000

Workings

Period to 30 September 2021

The profit to be allocated is £200,000 × 6/12 = £100,000 which is then split 4:1 as salaries are not paid in this period.

Period to 31 March 2022

The profit to be allocated is £200,000 × 6/12 = £100,000.

Salary is allocated to Tommy and Grace of £20,000 × 6/12 = £10,000 each, a total of £20,000.

The remaining profit to share in the profit sharing ratio is therefore £80,000 (£100,000 – £20,000). This is then split in the ratio 2:1:1.

(b) **Class 4 NICs**

	£
(£50,270 – £9,568) = £40,702 × 9%	3,663.18
(£62,000 – £50,270) = £11,730 × 2%	234.60
	3,897.78

(c) **Class 2 NICs**

	£
(£3.05 × 52 weeks)	158.60

Tutorial note

Self-employed taxpayers pay class 4 NICs based on their taxable trading profits in excess of £9,568 and the fixed rate class 2 NICs of £3.05 per week provided taxable trading profits exceed £6,515.

CHARGEABLE GAINS AND ALLOWABLE LOSSES OF COMPANIES

30 WENDYCO LTD

(a)

	True	False
Indexation allowance cannot create an allowable capital loss	✓	
If not all proceeds on the sale of an asset are reinvested in a new asset, the rollover relief will be equal to the amount of proceeds not reinvested		✓
Rollover relief claimed when an old building is sold and a new building bought reduces the base cost of the new building	✓	

Tutorial note

Indexation allowance cannot create nor increase a loss.

If not all proceeds are reinvested, the rollover relief is restricted. However, the amount of proceeds not reinvested is the amount chargeable (up to the amount of the gain), not the amount of the rollover relief.

(b) **Chargeable gain computation**

	£
Sale proceeds	500,000
Less: Cost	(120,000)
Enhancement expenditure (extension)	(80,000)
Less: Indexation allowance	(86,200)
(£120,000 × 0.669) = 80,280	
(£80,000 × 0.074) = 5,920	
	———
Chargeable gain	213,800
	———

Tutorial note

The redecoration costs are not capital costs and so are not deducted in the gains calculation.

The cost of the extension is indexed separately from the month the expenditure was incurred.

31 XYZ LTD

(a) **Chargeable gain computation**

	£
Sale proceeds	250,000
Less: Cost	(100,000)
Extension	(22,000)
	―――
Unindexed gain	128,000
Less: Indexation allowance	
(£100,000 × 0.315)	(31,500)
(£22,000 × 0.112)	(2,464)
	―――
Chargeable gain	94,036
	―――

Tutorial note

Roof repairs are not capital and cannot be deducted in the capital gains calculation.

Improvement costs such as the extension must be indexed separately. Indexation runs from the month in which the costs were incurred.

(b)

	True	False
For rollover relief to be available on the sale of a building, a new building must be bought		✓
Rollover relief cannot create a loss	✓	

Tutorial note

Rollover relief applies if the assets sold and bought are both qualifying assets but the assets do not need to be the same type e.g. both buildings.

Rollover relief can reduce a gain to nil but it cannot create a loss.

32   TOPHAM LTD

(a)   **Chargeable gain computation**

		£
Sale proceeds		42,000
Less: Cost		(40,000)
		2,000
Less: Indexation allowance (£40,000 × 0.080) = £3,200 restricted as cannot create a loss		(2,000)
Chargeable gain		0

Tutorial note

Indexation allowance runs from the month in which the costs were incurred up to December 2017 if the asset was sold on/after that date, but it cannot create an allowable loss.

(b)

	True	False
The relief is available on a sale of a qualifying asset if a qualifying replacement asset is bought within three years before or after the sale		✓
The base cost of a replacement building is reduced by the relief claimed	✓	
The relief is not available on the sale of a building which has always been rented out	✓	

Tutorial note

The replacement asset must be bought within three years after the sale or within one year before the sale.

Both the asset sold and the replacement asset must be used in the trade of the company for rollover relief to be available.

33   MALLC LTD

(a)   The gain chargeable before rollover relief is £306,400.

The gain chargeable after rollover relief is £135,000

The amount of rollover relief is £171,400

The base cost of the factory is £418,600

Working: Chargeable gain computation

	£
Sale proceeds	725,000
Less: Cost	(350,000)
Unindexed gain	375,000
Less: Indexation allowance (0.196 × £350,000)	(68,600)
Chargeable gain before rollover relief	306,400
Less: rollover relief – balancing figure (£306,400 – £135,000)	(171,400)
Chargeable gain (see below)	135,000

Chargeable at time of disposal = Lower of

(i)   Chargeable gain = £306,400

(ii)   Sale proceeds not reinvested = (£725,000 – £590,000) = £135,000

i.e. £135,000

Base cost of factory = (£590,000 – £171,400) = £418,600

(b)   A = 1 September 2020

B = 1 September 2024

Tutorial note

Rollover relief is available where an individual (not examinable) or a company

- *disposes of a qualifying business asset, and*
- *replaces with another qualifying business asset*
- *within 12 months before, and*
- *36 months after the date of disposal.*

If all of the sale proceeds are reinvested, the whole of the chargeable gain can be deferred.

If not all of the sale proceeds are reinvested, the chargeable gain now is the lower of the

(i)   chargeable gain, or

(ii)   sale proceeds not reinvested.

The remaining gain can be deferred with a rollover relief claim.

34   OLIVER LTD

(a)   (i)   The unindexed gain before rollover relief is £400,000.

(ii)   The indexation allowance is £181,500

(iii)   The amount of rollover relief is £168,500

Working: Chargeable gain computation

	£
Sale proceeds	800,000
Less: Cost	(300,000)
Less: Enhancement expenditure (extension)	(100,000)
Unindexed gain	400,000
Less: Indexation allowance on cost (0.605 × £300,000)	(181,500)
Chargeable gain before rollover relief	218,500
Less: rollover relief – balancing figure (£218,500 – £50,000)	(168,500)
Chargeable gain (see below)	50,000

Chargeable at time of disposal = Lower of

(i)   Chargeable gain = £218,500

(ii)   Sale proceeds not reinvested = (£800,000 – £750,000) = £50,000

i.e. £50,000

Tutorial note

The expenditure on the extension is an allowable deduction. As the expenditure was incurred after December 2017, there is no indexation allowance in respect of the extension.

Rollover relief is restricted as the entire proceeds on sale were not reinvested.

(iv)

	True	False
If the warehouse had been purchased in January 2021 rollover relief would have been available.	✓	
If Oliver Ltd had instead purchased fixed plant rather than the warehouse, rollover relief would have been available.	✓	
If Oliver Ltd had instead invested in shares in an unquoted trading company, rollover relief would have been available.		✓

Tutorial note

The replacement asset can be purchased within one year before the sale or within three years after the sale.

Fixed plant is a qualifying asset for rollover relief purposes.

Shares are not qualifying assets for the purposes of rollover relief.

35 ALLYNN LTD

(a) The chargeable gain before rollover relief is £1,308,600

The amount of rollover relief is £458,600

The base cost of the factory is £1,541,400

Working: Chargeable gain computation

	£
Sale proceeds	2,850,000
Less: Cost	(1,400,000)
Unindexed gain	1,450,000
Less: indexation allowance (0.101 × £1,400,000)	(141,400)
Chargeable gain before rollover relief	1,308,600
Less: rollover relief – balancing figure (£1,308,600 – £850,000)	(458,600)
Chargeable gain (see below)	850,000

Chargeable at time of disposal = Lower of

(i) Chargeable gain = £1,308,600

(ii) Sale proceeds not reinvested = (£2,850,000 – £2,000,000) = £850,000

i.e. £850,000

The base cost of the factory is (£2,000,000 – £458,600) = £1,541,400

(b) A = 1 February 2019

B = 1 February 2023

Tutorial note

Rollover relief is available where an individual or company

- *disposes of a qualifying business asset, and*
- *replaces with another qualifying business asset*
- *within 12 months before, and*
- *36 months after the date of disposal.*

If all of the sale proceeds are reinvested, the whole of the chargeable gain can be deferred.

If not all of the sale proceeds are reinvested, the chargeable gain now is the lower of the

(i)   chargeable gain, and

(ii)   sale proceeds not reinvested.

The remaining gain can be deferred with a rollover relief claim.

36   CHERY LTD

(a)   (i)   The allowable costs of sale are £7,000.

      (ii)   The allowable costs incurred in January 2018 are £2,853,000 (£2,600,000 + £3,000 + £250,000).

      (iii)   The allowable enhancement expenditure in March 2021 is £0.

Tutorial note

The legal fees incurred by the seller are allowable costs of sale. Costs paid by the purchaser are not allowable costs of sale.

The legal fees paid on purchase are also allowable costs. Expenditure required to be able to use the asset is capital expenditure and so allowable – here the cost of the roof.

Costs of painting windows and repairs are not capital items and so not allowable costs.

	True	False
(iv) Indexation allowance is available on the costs of purchase from January 2018 to February 2022.		✓
If a replacement office building were bought for £4,000,000 in March 2022 and let out, full rollover relief would be available.		✓
If a warehouse had been bought for £3,600,000 in May 2021 for use in the trade, partial rollover relief would be available.	✓	

Tutorial note

Indexation allowance is only available until December 2017.

An office building which is let out is not a qualifying asset for rollover relief. If the building is partially used for trade, partial rollover relief may be available.

The warehouse would be purchased within the time period of one year prior to sale, but the proceeds are not fully reinvested so partial rollover relief is available.

CALCULATING CHARGEABLE GAINS AND ALLOWABLE LOSSES IN COMPANY DISPOSAL OF SHARES

Key answer tips

Share disposals are tested in every assessment. The most commonly recurring error for disposals by companies is the handling of matching rules where shares are bought 9 days before the disposal. It is common for learners to ignore the matching rules completely and simply show one large pool that takes events in strict chronological order.

37 PUCK LTD

(a) **Share pool**

Transaction	Number of shares	Cost	Indexed cost
		£	£
June 2008	3,000	12,000	12,000
January 2012 Bonus issue (1 for 3)	1,000	0	0
	4,000	12,000	12,000
December 2015 Indexation update (£12,000 × 0.202)			2,424
Rights issue (1 for 4) at £2	1,000	2,000	2,000
	5,000	14,000	16,424
December 2017 Indexation update (£16,424 × 0.067)			1,100
	5,000	14,000	17,524
April 2021 – Disposal	(5,000)	(14,000)	(17,524)
Balance c/f	0	0	0

(b)   **Chargeable gain computation**

	£
Sale proceeds	24,000
Less: Cost (from part a)	(14,000)
Unindexed gain	10,000
Less: Indexation allowance (part a) (£17,524 – £14,000)	(3,524)
Chargeable gain	6,476

Tutorial note

Indexation is not required before recording a bonus issue, but is required before recording a rights issue and the disposal. When assets are sold on/after December 2017, indexation is only calculated up to December 2017.

Take care when reading the indexation information if it is presented in a table as in this question – you simply need to look up the row and column of the two dates and take the indexation factor from the relevant box – there is no need to do any calculations to establish the indexation factor.

38   PISTON LTD

(a)   **Share pool**

Transaction	Number of shares	Cost	Indexed cost
		£	£
August 2006	2,700	10,640	10,640
July 2013 Bonus issue (1 for 3)	900	0	0
	3,600	10,640	10,640
January 2014 Indexation update (£10,640 × 0.268)			2,852
Acquisition	2,300	7,130	7,130
	5,900	17,770	20,622
December 2017 Indexation update (£20,622 × 0.101)			2,083
			22,705
May 2021 – Disposal	(5,900)	(17,770)	(22,705)
Balance c/f	0	0	0

(b) **Chargeable gain computation**

	£
Sale proceeds	18,800
Less: Cost (from part a)	(17,770)
Unindexed gain	1,030
Less: Indexation allowance (part a) (£22,705 – £17,770)	
Restricted, indexation allowance cannot create a loss	(1,030)
Chargeable gain	0

Tutorial note

Indexation is not required before recording a bonus issue, but is required before recording the disposal.

Indexation allowance cannot turn a chargeable gain into a capital loss (or increase a capital loss).

39 DREAM LTD

(a) **Share pool**

Transaction	Number of shares	Cost	Indexed cost
		£	£
March 2000	6,000	12,000	12,000
June 2005 Bonus issue (1 for 2)	3,000	0	0
	9,000	12,000	12,000
January 2012 Indexation update (£12,000 × 0.413)			4,956
	9,000	12,000	16,956
January 2012 – Disposal (1,000/9,000) × £12,000 and £16,956	(1,000)	(1,333)	(1,884)
	8,000	10,667	15,072
December 2017 Indexation update (£15,072 × 0.168)			2,532
	8,000	10,667	17,604
December 2021 – Disposal (7,000/8,000) × £10,667 and £17,604	(7,000)	(9,334)	(15,404)
Balance c/f	1,000	1,333	2,200

Tutorial note

Indexation is not required before recording a bonus issue, but is required before recording the disposal.

(b) **Chargeable gain computation**

	£
Sale proceeds	46,350
Less: Cost (from part a)	(9,334)
Unindexed gain	37,016
Less: Indexation allowance (part a) (£15,404 – £9,334)	(6,070)
Chargeable gain	30,946

Tutorial note

There are two disposals but only the disposal in December 2021 is taxable in the year ended 31 December 2021 so only a gain on this disposal is required.

40 BATMAN LTD

(a) **Share pool**

Transaction	Number of shares	Cost	Indexed cost
		£	£
May 2006	7,000	14,000	14,000
July 2008 Bonus issue (1 for 8)	875	0	0
	7,875	14,000	14,000
July 2012 Indexation update (£14,000 × 0.225)			3,150
Rights issue (1 for 5) at £3	1,575	4,725	4,725
	9,450	18,725	21,875
December 2017 Indexation update (£21,875 × 0.149)			3,259
	9,450	18,725	25,134
September 2021 – Disposal (5,000/9,450) × £18,725 and £25,134	(5,000)	(9,907)	(13,298)
Balance c/f	4,450	8,818	11,836

Tutorial note

Indexation is not required before recording a bonus issue, but is required before recording the rights issue and the disposal.

(b)   **Chargeable gain computation**

	£
Sale proceeds (5,000 × £5)	25,000
Less: Cost (part a)	(9,907)
Unindexed gain	15,093
Less: Indexation allowance (part a) (£13,298 – £9,907)	(3,391)
Chargeable gain	11,702

41   SHELBYVILLE LTD

(a)   **Share pool**

Transaction	Number of shares	Cost	Indexed cost
		£	£
May 2017 Purchase	10,000	23,300	23,300
November 2017 Bonus issue (1 for 40)	250	0	0
	10,250	23,300	23,300
December 2017 Indexation update (£23,300 × 0.024)			559
	10,250	23,300	23,859
February 2022 – Disposal (3,875/10,250) × £23,300 and £23,859	(3,875)	(8,809)	(9,020)
Balance c/f	6,375	14,491	14,839

(b)   **Chargeable gain computation**

Disposal of 2,000 shares matched with the January 2022 purchase (in previous 9 days)	
	£
Sale proceeds (2,000 × £3.20)	6,400
Less: Cost	(5,950)
	———
Chargeable gain	450
	———
Disposal of 3,875 shares from the pool	
	£
Sale proceeds (3,875 × £3.20)	12,400
Less: Cost (from part a)	(8,809)
	———
Unindexed gain	3,591
Less: Indexation allowance (part a) (£9,020 – £8,809)	(211)
	———
Chargeable gain	3,380
	———
Total gains (£450 + £3,380)	3,830
	———

Tutorial note

The matching rules for a company specify that disposals of shares are matched with:

1   *purchases on the same day, and then*

2   *purchases in the previous 9 days (FIFO basis), and then*

3   *shares held in the share pool.*

Indexation is not required before recording a bonus issue, but is required before recording the disposal.

42   TREACOL LTD

(a)   **Share pool**

Transaction	Number of shares	Cost	Indexed cost
		£	£
May 2012	5,000	24,000	24,000
January 2016 Indexation update (£24,000 × 0.068)			1,632
Rights issue (1 for 2) at £6	2,500	15,000	15,000
	7,500	39,000	40,632
December 2017 Indexation update (£40,632 × 0.075)			3,047
	7,500	39,000	43,679
August 2021 – Disposal (3,000/7,500) × £39,000 and £43,679	(3,000)	(15,600)	(17,472)
Balance c/f	4,500	23,400	26,207

(b)   **Chargeable gain computation**

Disposal of 1,000 shares matched with the 2 August 2021 purchase (in previous 9 days)	
	£
Sale proceeds (1,000/4,000 × £32,000)	8,000
Less: Cost	(7,800)
Chargeable gain	200
Disposal of 3,000 shares from the pool	
	£
Sale proceeds (3,000/4,000 × £32,000)	24,000
Less: Cost (from part a)	(15,600)
Unindexed gain	8,400
Less: Indexation allowance (part a) (£17,472 – £15,600)	(1,872)
Chargeable gain	6,528
Total gains (£200 + £6,528)	6,728

Tutorial note

The matching rules for a company specify that disposals of shares are matched with:

1   *purchases on the same day, and then*

2   *purchases in the previous 9 days (FIFO basis), and then*

3   *shares held in the share pool.*

Indexation is required before recording a rights issue and before recording the disposal.

43   MAPPEL LTD

(a)   **Share pool**

Transaction	Number of shares	Cost	Indexed cost
		£	£
January 2004	8,000	36,000	36,000
June 2010 Indexation update (£36,000 × 0.224)			8,064
Purchase June 2010	2,000	12,000	12,000
	10,000	48,000	56,064
February 2012 Bonus issue (1 for 4)	2,500	0	0
	12,500	48,000	56,064
December 2017 Indexation update (£56,064 × 0.241)			13,511
	12,500	48,000	69,575
January 2019 – Disposal (5,000/12,500) × £48,000 and £69,575	(5,000)	(19,200)	(27,830)
	7,500	28,800	41,745
June 2021 – Disposal (3,000/7,500) × £28,800 and £41,745	(3,000)	(11,520)	(16,698)
Balance c/f	4,500	17,280	25,047

Tutorial note

Indexation is not required before recording a bonus issue, but is required before recording the purchase in June 2010 and up to December 2017 prior to the disposal.

(b)   **Chargeable gain computation**

	£
Sale proceeds	37,300
Less: Cost (part a)	(11,520)
Unindexed gain	25,780
Less: Indexation allowance (part a) (£16,698 – £11,520)	(5,178)
Chargeable gain	20,602

CALCULATING TAXABLE PROFITS AND CORPORATION TAX PAYABLE

44   WITHERS LTD

	£
Trading income	2,360,000
Investment income	3,000
Property income	110,000
Chargeable gains	230,000
Qualifying charitable donations	(20,000)
Taxable total profits	2,683,000
Corporation tax payable	509,770

Workings

Trading income = (£2,490,000 – £130,000) = £2,360,000

Tutorial note

Dividends received are not taxable.

45   MORGAN LTD

(a)   Answer = B

Tutorial note

A long period of account must be split into two accounting periods as follows:

Accounting period 1: First 12 months

Accounting period 2: Rest of the period.

(b)   **Corporation tax computation**

	£
Trading income	845,000
Investment income	0
Chargeable gains	57,000
Qualifying charitable donations	(10,000)
Taxable total profits	892,000
Corporation tax payable	169,480

Workings

Trading income = (£870,000 − £25,000) = £845,000

46   LONG LTD AND SHORT LTD

(a)

	Time apportion	Separate computation	Period in which it arises
Chargeable gains			✓
Capital allowances		✓	
Trading profits	✓		
Qualifying charitable donations			✓

(b)   **Corporation tax computation**

	£
Trading income	156,000
Investment income	1,000
Property income	0
Chargeable gains	20,000
Qualifying charitable donations	0
Taxable total profits	177,000
Corporation tax payable	33,630

47   SOIR LTD

(a)   Answer = B

Tutorial note

Qualifying charitable donations are deductible from total profits, not trading profits.

Dividend income should be excluded from TTP.

Chargeable gains should be included in TTP.

Capital allowances are deducted from trading profits, not total profits.

(b)   **Corporation tax computation**

	£
Trading income	236,700
Investment income	12,000
Chargeable gains	15,000
Qualifying charitable donations	(5,000)
Taxable total profits	258,700
Corporation tax payable	49,153

Workings

Trading income = (£230,000 + £6,700) = £236,700

48   COUPE LTD

	Total	First accounting period (12 months to 30 Sept 2021)	Second accounting period (3 months to 31 Dec 2021)
	£	£	£
Trading income before capital allowances	15,750	12,600	3,150
Capital allowances	7,000	(5,000)	(2,000)
Trading income after capital allowances		7,600	1,150
Rental income	7,500	6,000	1,500
Interest income	3,000	2,400	600
Chargeable gain	800	800	0
Qualifying charitable donation	1,000	0	(1,000)
Taxable total profits		16,800	2,250

Tutorial note

You first need to understand how the 15 month period is split – into a 12 month period ended 30 September 2021 and a 3 month period ended 31 December 2021.

Trading income is time apportioned.

Separate computations for each accounting period are required for capital allowances but the figures have been given here.

Interest income and rental income are allocated on an accruals basis.

Chargeable gains are allocated according to date of disposal and qualifying charitable donations according to the date of payment.

49 MERCURY LTD

Corporation tax payable – 9 months ended 31 March 2022

	£
Trading income (£250,000 + £5,700)	255,700
Investment income	1,000
Chargeable gains (£13,000 – £5,000)	8,000
Qualifying charitable donation	(2,000)
Taxable total profits	262,700
Corporation tax liability at 19%	49,913

Tutorial note

Trading income is reduced by capital allowances and increased by a balancing charge. Capital losses b/f are deducted from the chargeable gains. Dividend income is not taxable. Interest income is included in taxable total profits.

50 PANGOLIN LTD

Corporation tax payable – 16 month period ended 31 March 2022

	First accounting period	Second accounting period
	(Year ended 30 November 2021)	(Four months ended 31 March 2022)
	£	£
Trading profit (W)	56,900	18,400
Property income (12:4)	16,500	5,500
Chargeable gain	61,000	–
Qualifying charitable donation	(3,000)	–
Taxable total profits	131,400	23,900
Corporation tax liability at 19%	24,966	4,541

Workings

Trading profit is apportioned 12:4 before deducting capital allowances so:

Period 1 trading profit = (£80,000 × 12/16) – £3,100 = £56,900

Period 2 trading profit = (£80,000 × 4/16) – £1,600 = £18,400

Tutorial note

The capital allowances for the two periods have already been calculated separately and these are deducted after apportioning the trading profits between the two periods.

THE ADMINISTRATIVE REQUIREMENTS FOR UK TAX LAW

Key answer tips

When asked for dates it is important to identify the full date, including the year, and to ensure that it is the right year! Unfortunately, if one date is wrong, they tend to all be wrong.

When calculating payments on account, you must remember which year the payments should be based on, ensure that you know what is included in the payments on account system and what is payable as part of the balancing payment. You should ensure that you state accurate dates.

Regarding penalties, it is important to be clear about which penalties apply to which offence as they all have different penalty systems – late payment and late filing in particular, but also incorrect filing and failure to keep records. The chief assessor has commented in the past that it is very common for learners to give the penalties that apply to late filing in answer to a question about late payment and vice versa. This usually results in no marks being allocated to a question on this topic.

51 IRFAN

   (a)   (i)   31 January 2022

           (ii)   31 January 2023

           (iii) 31 January 2023

           (iv) 31 July 2022

Tutorial note

A self-employed individual must pay 'Payments on account' for income tax and class 4 NICs, based on the previous year's income tax and class 4 NICs payable, on 31 January in the tax year and 31 July following the end of the tax year.

The final balancing payment is due on 31 January following the end of the tax year.

Capital gains tax is not paid in instalments, it is all due on 31 January following the end of the tax year.

(b)

	True	False
An individual must retain tax records for his/her business for 2021/22 until 5 April 2024		✓
If an individual is seven months late in submitting the tax return for 2021/22, he/she will receive a maximum penalty of £200		✓
The maximum penalty for a mistake in a tax return due to carelessness is 70%		✓
If an individual's balancing payment for 2021/22 is two months late he/she can be charged a penalty for late payment of 5%	✓	
A company with a period of account ending 30 September 2021 must submit its tax return by 30 September 2022	✓	
Interest is charged on late payments of balancing payments and instalments	✓	

Tutorial note

An individual's business records must be retained for five years after the filing date (i.e. 31 January following the end of the tax year). Therefore, the 2021/22 records must be kept until 31 January 2028.

The penalties for an individual filing a tax return late are as follows:

(i)   *Within three months of the due date = £100 fixed penalty*

(ii)   *Between three to six months of the due date = Additional daily penalties of £10 per day (Maximum 90 days)*

(iii) *Between six to 12 months of due date = Additional 5% of tax due (Minimum £300)*

(iv)   *More than 12 months after the due date = Additional 5% of tax due (Minimum £300)*

(v)   *More than 12 months after the due date if the taxpayer withholds information:*

–   *deliberate and concealed = 100% (Minimum £300)*

–   *deliberate and not concealed = 70% (Minimum £300).*

The maximum penalty for incorrect returns depends on the behaviour of the taxpayer, and is calculated as a percentage of tax lost as follows:

(i)   *Mistake despite taking reasonable care – no penalty*

(ii)   *Failure to take reasonable care – 30%*

(iii) *Deliberate understatement – 70%*

(iv)   *Deliberate understatement with concealment – 100%.*

In addition to tax and possible interest, late payment penalties are applied to unpaid tax. However, late payment penalties only apply to the final payment of income tax, class 2 and 4 NICs and capital gains tax.

The amount due is:

(i)   5% of the unpaid tax if it is more than one month late

(ii)   A further 5% if more than six months late

(iii)   A further 5% if more than 12 months late.

A company must submit its tax return within 12 months of the end of the accounting period.

Interest is payable on any tax paid late.

(c)   (i)   The date by which Diamon Ltd had to inform HMRC of the start of its first accounting period is 30 June 2019.

        (ii)   The due date for payment of Diamon Ltd's corporation tax liability for the year ended 31 March 2020 is 1 January 2021.

        (iii)   The latest date that HMRC could have opened an enquiry into the return for the year ended 31 March 2020 was 28 February 2022.

        (iv)   The minimum percentage of potential lost revenue that could be charged as a penalty in respect of the error is 50%.

        (v)   If Diamon Ltd did not keep proper records for the year ended 31 March 2020, the company is liable to a penalty of £3,000.

Tutorial note

The company must inform HMRC within three months of the start of its first accounting period.

The augmented profits are below the limit of £1,500,000 and so quarterly instalment payments are not required.

For an individual company, HMRC may raise an enquiry up to 12 months from the submission of the return.

A deliberate and concealed error has a maximum penalty of 100% of potential lost revenue, but this may be reduced to 50% where the error is prompted. The error is prompted here by the enquiry.

The penalty for failure to keep records is £3,000.

52   PAYMENTS AND PENALTIES

(a)   **Payments on account**

	True	False
POAs are not required if the income tax and class 4 NIC payable for the previous year by self-assessment is less than £1,000	✓	
POAs for 2021/22 are due on 31 July 2022 and 31 January 2023		✓
POAs are not required if more than 80% of the income tax and capital gains tax liability for the previous year was met through tax deducted under PAYE		✓
POAs of class 2 NICs are never required	✓	
POAs of class 4 NICs are optional; the taxpayer can choose to pay under monthly direct debit or quarterly invoice if they prefer		✓

Tutorial note

POAs are not required if:

(i)   the total amount of income tax and class 4 NICs payable for the previous year after the deduction of tax under PAYE is less than £1,000, or

(ii)   more than 80% of the income tax and class 4 NICs liability for the previous year was met through tax deducted at source.

Capital gains tax is not taken into account when deciding whether POAs are required.

POAs are not optional. Unless the conditions above apply, POAs must be paid.

POAs are due on 31 January in the tax year (i.e. 31 January 2022) and 31 July following the end of the tax year (i.e. 31 July 2022) for 2021/22.

(b)   (i)   14 April 2022

      (ii)   1 October 2022

      (iii) 1 November 2022

      (iv)   14 October 2021

Tutorial note

(i)   *The augmented profits limit of £1,500,000 is reduced to £750,000 (£1,500,000 × 6/12) for the six month period. With a revised limit of £750,000 and augmented profits of £900,000, the company is 'large'. The first payment is due on 14th of the 7th month following the start of the accounting period, which in this case is the first month of the next accounting period.*

(ii)   *With an augmented profits limit of £1,125,000 (£1,500,000 × 9/12) for the short accounting period and augmented profits of £900,000, the company is not 'large'. The due date for its tax liability is nine months and one day after the end of the accounting period.*

(iii)   *With an augmented profits limit of £1,500,000 and augmented profits of £900,000, the company is not 'large'. The due date for its tax liability is nine months and one day after the end of the accounting period.*

(iv)   *With an augmented profits limit of £875,000 (£1,500,000 × 7/12) and augmented profits of £900,000, the company is 'large'. The first payment is always due on 14th of the 7th month following the start of the accounting period, regardless of the length of the accounting period.*

(c)   (i)   B

         (ii)   C

         (iii)   A

         (iv)   A

Tutorial note

Penalties for submitting a company's tax return late are as follows:

(i)   *Within three months of the due date = £100 fixed penalty*

(ii)   *Between three to six months of the due date = £200 fixed penalty*

(iii)   *Between six to 12 months of due date = Additional 10% of tax due*

(iv)   *More than 12 months after the due date = Additional 20% of tax due*

The maximum penalty for incorrect returns depends on the behaviour of the taxpayer, and is calculated as a percentage of tax lost as follows:

(i)   *Mistake despite taking reasonable care – no penalty*

(ii)   *Failure to take reasonable care – 30%*

(iii)   *Deliberate understatement – 70%*

(iv)   *Deliberate understatement with concealment – 100%.*

53   NAGINA

    (a)   (i)   31 July 2022

           (ii)   31 October 2022

           (iii) 1 October 2022

           (iv) Large/Current

Tutorial note

A self-employed individual must pay 'payments on account' for income tax and class 4 NICs based on the previous years' income tax payable and class 4 liability on:

(i)   31 January in the tax year, and

(ii)   31 July following the end of the tax year.

An individual can choose to file his/her return either on paper or electronically online:

(i)   If filing on paper, the due date is 31 October following the end of the tax year.

(ii)   Electronic filing must be submitted by 31 January following the end of the tax year.

The normal due date for corporation tax is nine months and one day after the end of the accounting period.

However, where the company is 'large' (i.e. its augmented profits exceed the £1,500,000 augmented profits limit), it must pay its corporation tax by quarterly instalments based on the estimated corporation tax liability for the current year.

    (b)

	True	False
The maximum penalty for a sole trader failing to keep records is £3,000 per accounting period	✓	
The maximum penalty for a failure by an individual to notify chargeability is 100% of the tax due but unpaid	✓	
A late payment penalty can apply to payments on account of income tax		✓
Companies can choose whether to file paper tax returns or file online		✓

Tutorial note

The maximum penalty for notifying chargeability depends on the behaviour of the taxpayer, and is calculated in broadly the same way as the penalty for an incorrect return.

The late payment penalty only applies to the final payments of income tax and class 4 NICs and to the payment of class 2 NICs and capital gains tax, not payments on account.

Companies must file their returns online.

(c)   (i)   C

Tutorial note

HMRC must issue a written notice to initiate a compliance check and cannot issue a notice more than 12 months after the date the return was actually filed.

(ii)

	True	False
If Jane fails to produce documents during an enquiry, she may suffer a £300 penalty	✓	
If Jane tells HMRC about a careless error in her 2020/21 return during an enquiry, the penalty can be reduced to nil		✓
Interest is only payable on a late balancing payment, not late payments on account		✓
If Jane submits her 2021/22 tax return on 20 January 2023, she will have until 31 January 2024 to make an amendment	✓	

Tutorial note

The penalty for a careless error can be reduced to nil but only if the disclosure to HMRC is unprompted. Disclosure during an enquiry would be prompted with a minimum penalty of 15%.

Interest is payable on late payments on account and on late balancing payments. Only a late balancing payment gives rise to a penalty, however.

A taxpayer can make an amendment with 12 months of the due filing date (not the actual date submitted).

54   MANINDER

(a)   (i)   31 March 2023

(ii)   1 January 2023

(iii)   14 October 2021

(iv)   14 July 2022

Tutorial note

The normal due date for corporation tax is nine months and one day after the end of the accounting period.

However, where the company is large (i.e. has augmented profits above £1,500,000), it must pay its corporation tax by quarterly instalments.

The instalments are due on the 14th day of the 7th, 10th, 13th and 16th month after the start of the accounting period.

(b)

	True	False
The filing deadline for electronic submission of an individual's 2021/22 tax return is 31 January 2023	✓	
A self-employed individual is required to keep records to support his/her 2021/22 tax return until 31 January 2028	✓	
There is no penalty for late submission of an individual's tax return as long as it is less than six months late		✓
If a company makes a mistake in the tax return due to failure to take reasonable care, there is a penalty of up to 30%	✓	
An individual should make the first payment on account for 2021/22 on 31 January 2023		✓

Tutorial note

An individual can choose to file the tax return either on paper or electronically online:

(i)   *If filing on paper, the due date is 31 October following the end of the tax year.*

(ii)   *Electronic filing must be submitted by 31 January following the end of the tax year.*

An individual's business records must be retained for five years after the filing date (i.e. 31 January following the end of the tax year). Therefore, the 2021/22 records must be kept until 31 January 2028.

Penalties for submitting an individual's tax return late are as follows:

(i)   *Within three months of the due date = £100 fixed penalty*

(ii)   *Between three to six months of the due date = Additional daily penalties of £10 per day (Maximum 90 days)*

(iii)   *Between six to 12 months of due date = Additional 5% of tax due (Minimum £300)*

(iv)   *More than 12 months after the due date = Additional 5% of tax due (Minimum £300)*

(v)   More than 12 months after the due date if the taxpayer withholds information:

–   deliberate and concealed = 100% (Minimum £300)

–   deliberate and not concealed = 70% (Minimum £300).

The maximum penalty for a company making a mistake on their return depends on the behaviour of the company, and is calculated as a percentage of tax lost as follows:

(i)   Mistake despite taking reasonable care – no penalty

(ii)   Failure to take reasonable care – 30%

(iii)   Deliberate understatement – 70%

(iv)   Deliberate understatement with concealment – 100%.

A self-employed individual must pay 'Payments on account' for income tax and class 4 NICs based on the previous year's results on:

(i)   31 January in the tax year, and

(ii)   31 July following the end of the tax year.

(c)

	True	False
If an individual is eight months late in submitting the tax return for 2021/22, he/she will receive a penalty of £200		✓
The maximum penalties for errors made by individuals in their tax returns vary from 20% to 100%		✓
If a company fails to keep records for the appropriate period of time, it can be fined up to £2,000		✓
A company with a period of account ending on 30 June 2021, must keep its records until 30 June 2029		✓
Late payment penalties are not normally imposed on payments on account	✓	

Tutorial note

Penalties for submitting an individual's tax return late are as follows:

(i)   Within three months of the due date = £100 fixed penalty

(ii)   Between three to six months of the due date = Additional daily penalties of £10 per day (Maximum 90 days)

(iii)   Between six to 12 months of due date = Additional 5% of tax due (Minimum £300) *(iv)* More than 12 months after the due date = Additional 5% of tax due (Minimum £300)

(v) More than 12 months after the due date if the taxpayer withholds information:

– deliberate and concealed = 100% (Minimum £300)

– deliberate and not concealed = 70% (Minimum £300).

The maximum penalty for errors made by an individual in his/her tax return depends on the behaviour of the taxpayer, and is calculated as a percentage of tax lost as follows:

(i) Mistake despite taking reasonable care – no penalty

(ii) Failure to take reasonable care – 30%

(iii) Deliberate understatement – 70%

(iv) Deliberate understatement with concealment – 100%.

Companies must keep records until six years from the end of the accounting period.

The maximum penalty for a company failing to keep records is £3,000 per accounting period affected.

Late payment penalties only apply to the final payment of income tax, class 2 and 4 NICs and capital gains tax, not payments on account.

55 LAREDO

(a)

	True	False
All tax records for an individual should be kept for at least four years.		✓
The maximum penalty for not keeping records is £2,000.		✓
An individual whose income tax and class 4 NICs payable by self-assessment for the previous tax year is less than £1,000 is not required to make payments on account.	✓	
Tax on chargeable gains is paid in two instalments on 31 January in the tax year and 31 July following the end of the tax year.		✓

Tutorial note

Tax records should be kept for one year from 31 January following the tax year for personal records and five years for business records.

Taxpayers can be fined up to £3,000 for failure to keep records.

There are no instalments for capital gains tax.

The whole of the capital gains tax liability is due on 31 January following the end of the tax year (i.e. 31 January 2023 for the 2021/22 tax year).

(b) (i) The total income tax and class 4 NICs due on 31 July 2022 is £3,035

(ii) The total income tax and class 4 NICs due on 31 January 2023 is £7,385

(iii) The amount of class 2 NICs due on 31 July 2022 is £0

(iv) The amount of class 2 NICs due on 31 January 2023 is £159

Working

31 July 2022

	£
Income tax liability for 2020/21	4,000
Class 4 liability for 2020/21	2,070
Liability for 2020/21	6,070
Second payment on account for 2021/22 £6,070/2	3,035

31 January 2023

	£
Income tax liability for 2021/22	6,000
Class 4 liability for 2021/22	2,970
Liability for 2021/22	8,970
Less: POA for 2021/22 (from above)	(6,070)
Balancing payment for 2021/22	2,900
First payment on account for 2022/23 £8,970/2	4,485
Total income tax and class 4 NICs due on 31 January 2023	7,385

Tutorial note

A self-employed individual must pay 'Payments on account' for income tax and class 4 NICs, based on the previous year's income tax and class 4 NICs payable, on 31 January in the tax year and 31 July following the end of the tax year.

The final balancing payment is due on 31 January following the end of the tax year.

Class 2 is paid on 31 January following the end of the tax year.

(c) (i) In respect of the year ended 31 December 2020 the first payment of corporation tax is due by 14 July 2020.

(ii) The amount payable by that date is £85,500 (£342,000/4).

(iii) In respect of the period ended 30 September 2021 the first payment of corporation tax is due by 1 July 2022

(iv) The amount payable by that date is £190,000.

Tutorial note

The normal due date for corporation tax is nine months and one day after the end of the accounting period.

However, where the company is large (i.e. has augmented profits above £1,500,000), it must pay its corporation tax by quarterly instalments. This is the case for the year ended 31 December 2020 here.

The instalments are due on the 14th day of the 7th, 10th, 13th and 16th month after the start of the accounting period.

The limit for instalments is reduced for a short accounting period, being £1,125,000 (£1,500,000 × 9/12) for the period ended 30 September 2021. The company is not large in that period.

56   AMIR

(a)   (i)   Amir should have notified HMRC of his chargeability by 5 October 2021.

(ii)   Amir should have submitted his 2020/21 tax return online by 31 January 2022.

(iii)   Amir should have paid his income tax and NIC liabilities for 2020/21 by 31 January 2022.

(iv)   Amir's late filing penalty is £100

(v)   Amir's late payment penalty if £173 (£3,450 × 5%)

Tutorial note

An individual must notify HMRC of chargeability by 5 October following the tax year.

An individual can choose to file his/her return either on paper or electronically online:

(i)   If filing on paper, the due date is 31 October following the end of the tax year.

(ii)   Electronic filing must be submitted by 31 January following the end of the tax year.

A self-employed individual must pay 'payments on account' for income tax and class 4 NICs based on the previous years' income tax payable and class 4 liability on:

(i)   31 January in the tax year, and

(ii)   31 July following the end of the tax year.

The balancing payment is due on 31 January following the end of the tax year.

POAs are not required if:

(i)   the total amount of income tax and class 4 NICs payable for the previous year after the deduction of tax under PAYE is less than £1,000, or

(ii)   more than 80% of the income tax and class 4 NICs liability for the previous year was met through tax deducted at source.

Penalties for submitting an individual's tax return late are as follows:

(i)   Within three months of the due date = £100 fixed penalty

(ii)   Between three to six months of the due date = Additional daily penalties of £10 per day (Maximum 90 days)

(iii) Between six to 12 months of due date = Additional 5% of tax due (Minimum £300)

(iv)   More than 12 months after the due date = Additional 5% of tax due (Minimum £300)

(v)   More than 12 months after the due date if the taxpayer withholds information:

–   deliberate and concealed = 100% (Minimum £300)

–   deliberate and not concealed = 70% (Minimum £300).

Penalties for a late balancing payment are:

(i)   5% of the unpaid tax if it is more than one month late

(ii)   A further 5% if more than six months late

(iii) A further 5% if more than 12 months late

(b)

	True	False
Lamb Ltd has paid all four quarterly instalment payments late for the year ended 31 December 2021.		✓
Lamb Ltd pays interest on the late payment of corporation tax.	✓	
Lamb Ltd's augmented profits exceed £1,500,000 for the year ended 31 December 2021.	✓	
Lamb Ltd should have made quarterly instalments based on 25% of the corporation tax liability for the previous year.		✓

Tutorial note

Where the company is large (i.e. has augmented profits above £1,500,000), it must pay its corporation tax by quarterly instalments.

The instalments are due on the 14th day of the 7th, 10th, 13th and 16th month after the start of the accounting period. Only three payments are late here as the final payment is due by 14 April 2022.

The instalments are based on the estimate liability for the current period.

(c)   (i)   Roger may amend his 2020/21 tax return at any point until 31 January 2023

(ii)   Roger must pay his first payment on account of income tax for 2021/22 by 31 January 2022

(iii) Roger must pay his class 2 national insurance contributions for 2021/22 by 31 January 2023

(iv)   Roger must keep records in respect of his 2020/21 tax return until 31 January 2027

Tutorial note

A taxpayer can make an amendment with 12 months of the due filing date (not the actual date submitted).

Class 2 NIC is paid by 31 January following the end of the tax year.

An individual's business records must be retained for five years after the filing date (i.e. 31 January following the end of the tax year). Therefore, the 2020/21 records must be kept until 31 January 2027.

57   SHEP LTD

(a)   (i)   The corporation tax payment due date was 1 January 2021.

(ii)   The corporation tax return filing due date was 31 March 2021.

(iii)   The fixed rate penalty for late filing of the tax return was £200.

(iv)   The tax-geared penalty for late filing of the tax return is £7,600.

Tutorial note

The corporation tax return was submitted over six months late.

Penalties for submitting a company's tax return late are as follows:

(i)   Within three months of the due date = £100 fixed penalty

(ii)   Between three to six months of the due date = £200 fixed penalty

(iii)   Between six to 12 months of due date = Additional 10% of tax due

(iv)   More than 12 months after the due date = Additional 20% of tax due

(b)   (i)   The minimum penalty is £0.

(ii)   The minimum penalty is 15% of potential lost revenue.

(iii)   He may be liability to a penalty of £3,000.

(iv)   Sandra may also incur a daily penalty of £60.

(v)   The maximum penalty is 100% of potential lost revenue.

Tutorial note

If the taxpayer files an incorrect tax return, a penalty equal to a percentage of the tax under declared may be charged. The penalty may be waived for inadvertent errors, as long as the taxpayer notifies HMRC of the error as soon as possible.

The percentage depends on the reason for the error.

Taxpayer behaviour	Maximum penalty (% of tax lost)
Mistake despite taking reasonable care	No penalty
Failure to take reasonable care	30%
Deliberate understatement	70%
Deliberate understatement with concealment	100%

The penalties may be reduced at HMRC discretion, depending on the type of penalty and whether the taxpayer makes an unprompted disclosure of the error.

Making an unprompted error of a careless error (as Sophie has done) reduces the error to nil.

A disclosure of an error during an enquiry is a prompted error. The penalty for the error in Ash Ltd is therefore reduced to 15% – it is likely to be considered careless especially as the financial controller would have noticed the difference from previous years if care had been taken.

The finance director of Noirt Ltd makes a deliberate error. By changing the invoice she also conceals the error, hence the maximum penalty of 100%.

Taxpayers can be fined up to £3,000 for failure to keep records.

The penalty for failure to produce documents for an enquiry is £300 plus possible penalties of £60 per day.

(c)

	True	False
Janine does not submit her income tax return earlier than the due date as doing so would give HMRC longer to raise an enquiry into the return.		✓
A company which is not large pays its corporation tax 11 months after the end of the accounting period. The company will be charged a penalty of 5%.		✓
A large company pays quarterly instalments based on an estimate of the corporation tax liability for that period.	✓	
The maximum penalty for late filing of an income tax return is 100% of the tax due.	✓	

Tutorial note

HMRC have 12 months from the actual date of submission to open an enquiry, so early submission does not extend the enquiry window.

Companies pay interest on late payments of corporation tax, but not penalties.

TAX PLANNING AND THE RESPONSIBILITIES OF THE BUSINESS AND AGENT

Key answer tips

To answer a written question, you must make sure you have understood the scenario you are being asked about, and that your answer is specific to that situation and not just generalised facts. The chief assessor comments that often learners give very generic, basic answers that may be technically correct, but are not directly related to the scenario given.

58   LEANNE

(a)   (i)   Leanne's action is tax planning as setting a dividend level to avoid higher rate tax is a legal way to reduce tax. It is not tax avoidance as Leanne is using tax law as it was intended rather than exploiting loopholes.

It is not tax evasion as she is not deliberately misleading HMRC by suppressing information or providing false information to reduce her tax liability.

(ii)   An accountant cannot share information about a client with other clients or with HMRC, unless the client gives permission.

Tutorial note

The ethical principle of confidentiality means the accountant cannot share information without permission, except with the client herself.

(b)   **Whether Melanie will be treated as carrying on a trade**

An item of furniture could be a trading asset or an investment or for personal use so the 'subject matter' test is inconclusive.

Melanie is an investment banker. Restoring and selling furniture is not similar to any trading activity carried on by Melanie.

The work carried out by Melanie in restoring the furniture may indicate that Melanie is trading as she is adding value to the asset.

The method of acquisition for the original furniture is inheritance which is unlikely to suggest trading.

So far Melanie has sold the furniture she inherited, but if she starts buying and selling frequently this would be trading.

Melanie's motive in purchasing more furniture to renovate and sell is partly to make a profit, which is indicative of trading.

Therefore, overall it is unlikely that the Melanie was trading when she sold the items of furniture she **inherited**. However, in terms of the additional items of furniture **purchased** by Melanie for renovation and sale Melanie is likely to be regarded as trading.

Tutorial note

In order to decide if an individual is trading it is often useful to look at the 'badges of trade'. These are tests which were originally developed by a Royal Commission in the 1950s and have been further developed by case law over the years.

The badges of trade are:

– *Subject matter (S)*

– *Length of ownership (O)*

– *Frequency of transactions (F)*

– *Improvements or supplementary work (I)*

– *Circumstances of realisation (R)*

– *Profit motive (M)*

The following additional badges are also considered:

– *The source of finance (F)*

– *Method of acquisition (A)*

– *Existence of similar trading transactions (ST)*

You should make sure you refer to the specific facts in the scenario and link them to these badges of trade. You would not have to make all the points given in the answer above to achieve full marks.

It is important that you draw a conclusion as you have been asked whether the individual is trading. Here there are two aspects to the activity, part of which is likely not to be trading and part of which is a trading activity. Your answer should make that clear.

(c)   **Payment of a dividend**

A dividend is not a deductible expense against trading profit for corporation tax and so can only be paid out of profits after corporation tax at 19% has been charged. This means the maximum dividend is £24,300 (£30,000 − (£30,000 × 19%)). There is no employer's national insurance contributions (NIC) on a dividend.

Ahmed's total income on receipt of this dividend is £42,300 (£10,000 + £8,000 + £24,300). After deduction of the personal allowance of £12,570, this is within the basic rate band of £37,700 and so the dividend will be taxed at 7.5%. Ahmed does not pay NIC on the dividend. Ahmed will receive £22,477 (£24,300 − (£24,300 × 7.5%)).

Payment of additional salary

Additional salary is a deductible expense for corporation tax. The full £30,000 can be paid out but this must also cover the employer's NIC charged at 13.8% which is also deductible from trading profits.

The additional salary received by Ahmed is £26,362 (£30,000/1.138).

Ahmed's additional salary is within his basic rate band and so the income tax on the salary is charged at 20%. Ahmed also pays NIC on this amount at 12%. Ahmed keeps an amount of £17,926 after tax and NIC (£26,262 − (£26,362 × 32%)).

Tutorial note

You would not need to include all the calculations shown above to achieve full marks for this question. However, you must relate your comments to the facts of the scenario including reference to the appropriate rates. For example, you must give the correct rates for the income tax on the dividend and additional salary, recognising that the amounts will fall in the basic rate band. Stating all income tax rates for these types of income is unlikely to score any marks.

Work methodically through the two options for extracting profit. Consider first the corporation tax implications. Then any employer's national insurance implications. Then the income tax and national insurance implications for the individual.

59 STUART

(a) (i) Tax evasion is deliberately misleading HMRC by suppressing information or providing false information to reduce a tax liability. It is illegal.

Tax avoidance is a legal means of reducing a tax liability by exploiting loopholes or using tax law in a way that was not intended.

(ii) Stuart's action is tax evasion as he is deliberately overstating his expenditure in his capital allowance claim in his tax return to reduce his tax liability.

Tutorial note

Tax evasion (such as deliberately failing to disclose all of your income or taking an excessive relief) is illegal.

Tax avoidance uses legal means to reduce your tax bill. Tax avoidance is acting within the law but against the spirit of the law.

(b) Clara would disclose information about a client if authority has been given by the client, or if there is a legal, regulatory or professional right or duty to disclose. The duty of confidentiality also relates to dealings with HMRC. However, Clara must ensure that, whilst acting in the client's best interests, she consults with HMRC staff in an open and constructive manner.

(c) Clara's greatest duty of care is to her client.

(d) **Misha's choice of business structure**

Sole trader business

Misha is charged to income tax on the trading profits of the business, regardless of how much profit she extracts from the business. In the first year, there will be no income tax as the level of profits is below the personal allowance of £12,570. As her trading profits increase to £50,000, trading profits above the personal allowance will be taxed at 20%.

Misha will pay class 2 national insurance contributions (NICs) of £3.05 per week from the first year, as her trading profits will exceed £6,515.

Misha will pay class 4 NICs on trading profits above £9,568 at 9%, again regardless of how much profit she extracts.

Company

Corporation tax of 19% is charged on trading profits, whatever the level of profits.

Misha could take profits as a dividend. In the first year this would be covered by her personal allowance and no income tax is payable. There is no NIC in relation to the dividend. When profits increase to £50,000, the maximum rate of income tax on the dividends is 7.5% as the dividend will fall within the basic rate band.

Alternatively, the company could pay Misha a salary. Salaries above a lower limit are charged to employer's NIC at 13.8%. Both the salary and employer's NIC are deductible from trading profits so reduce the company's corporation tax, to nil if the entire profits are withdrawn like this.

Misha will pay NICs on salary above £9,568 at 12%. Initially, she will pay no income tax as the maximum salary will be below the personal allowance. When the salary exceeds this, she will pay income tax at 20%.

Tutorial note

You may be asked to compare possible business structures. Remember that you are given the figures for profits for a reason – make sure your explanations refer to the rates relevant to these levels of profits. Here, two different levels are given suggesting there may be a difference in the tax implications in the two cases. In this case, the personal allowance means there is no income tax in the lower level scenario. Don't forget NICs, and remember that these do not apply to dividend income.

60 SAKI AND IAN

(a) (i) You must get written authorisation/permission from Saki before disclosing her information to her husband. This is because of the fundamental principle of confidentiality, meaning that information about a client cannot be disclosed to another person.

   (ii) The same action would be required if the bank had approached the accountancy firm directly.

Tutorial note

An accountant generally needs the client's permission before revealing confidential information.

(b)   **Tax planning opportunities for civil partners**

Charmaine does not currently use all of her personal allowance. If the building society deposits held by Judith are transferred to Charmaine, the interest would suffer no income tax rather than tax at a rate of up to 40%.

If the company were to employ Charmaine, there would be a deduction for corporation tax purposes only if the level of Charmaine's salary is reasonable for the work she does. This would then save corporation tax at 19%.

The proposed salary is £4,800 (12 × 400). This amount is below the lower limits for national insurance contributions by the company and by Charmaine.

The salary is also below £5,570 (£12,570 – £5,000 – £2,000), so even if the deposits are transferred to Charmaine, her income is still covered by the personal allowance and no income tax is payable either.

If the couple want to maintain the same take-home pay between them, Judith could reduce her salary by a similar amount, saving income tax at 40% and NIC at 2%. The employer's NIC at 13.8% would also decrease (with a slight increase in corporation tax because of this).

Tutorial note

Spouses or civil partners may plan so that both use their personal allowance and their basic rate bands, in preference to one receiving all income and paying tax at a higher rate.

(c)   **Differences in taxation between company and sole trader business**

As a sole trader, Oli will be taxed on the additional £40,000 profits even though she will not draw the amount from the business. Income tax will be charged at 40% and NICs at 2% as Oli's existing income exceeds £50,270.

Tamar trades through a company and so corporation tax at 19% will be charged on the profits. As Tamar will not extract these profits there is no income tax or NICs.

Tutorial note

The sole trader suffers income tax and NICs regardless of the level of drawings, and so here suffers much higher tax than the trader who retains profits in a company.

61 FRED

(a) The nature of the asset is such that it could be held for personal enjoyment, as an investment or for trading purposes. Fred bought the painting to enjoy at home.

He has only sold one painting in a seven year period, so has not undertaken frequent transactions expected in a trade. The interval between purchase and sale is also long, not indicating trading.

Fred does not have a profit seeking motive in buying and selling the painting but is selling as he wants the funds to buy a house.

Fred is a lawyer and does not appear to carry on any other activities relating to trade in art.

Fred does work on the item prior to sale to make it more marketable which might be considered part of a trading activity. However, making a repair is reasonable to achieve the best price on sale of an investment.

A specialist art magazine may be used by collectors or traders so this method of sale does not indicate a trade.

Fred would not be carrying on a trade by selling this painting.

Tutorial note

Remember to refer to specific badges of trade and the facts of the scenario.

The badges of trade are:

Subject matter (S)

Length of ownership (O)

Frequency of transactions (F)

Improvements or supplementary work (I)

Circumstances of realisation (R)

Profit motive (M)

The following additional badges are also considered:

The source of finance (F)

Method of acquisition (A)

Existence of similar trading transactions (ST)

(b) (i) Tax planning is using legal methods of reducing a tax liability, in the way that the law is intended.

Tax avoidance is a legal means of reducing a tax liability by exploiting loopholes or using tax law in a way that was not intended.

Tax evasion is deliberately misleading HMRC by suppressing information or providing false information to reduce a tax liability. It is illegal.

(ii) Jessica would be involved in tax avoidance if she participates in the scheme.

(iii) The accountancy firm must first seek written permission from Jessica before providing another company with information about Jessica's trading profits.

Tutorial note

The scheme is legal but exploits a loophole in the law and so is an example of tax avoidance.

An accountant generally needs the client's permission before revealing confidential information.

(c) **Payment of a dividend**

A dividend is not a deductible expense against trading profit for corporation tax and so can only be paid out of profits after corporation tax at 19% has been charged. This means the maximum dividend from the additional profits is £12,150 (£15,000 − (£15,000 × 19%)). There are no employer's national insurance contributions (NICs) on a dividend.

Motsi's existing income from the company exceeds £50,270 (the personal allowance plus basic rate band) meaning she pays tax at the higher rate on further income. The income tax on the dividend income is 32.5% and there is no NIC so Motsi would receive £8,201 (£12,150 − (£12,150 × 32.5%)).

Payment of additional salary

Additional salary is a deductible expense for corporation tax. The full £15,000 can be paid out but this must also cover the employer's NIC charged at 13.8% which is also deductible from trading profits.

The additional salary received by Motsi is £13,181 (£15,000/1.138).

The income tax charged on this is at 40% and Motsi must also pay NICs on this amount at 12%. Motsi keeps an amount of £6,327 after tax and NICs (£13,181 − (£13,181 × 52%)).

Tutorial note

You would not need to include all the calculations shown above to achieve full marks for this question. However, you must relate your comments to the facts of the scenario including reference to the appropriate rates.

The taxpayer has already received an amount of salary and dividends – you only need to consider the tax implications of an additional profit withdrawal. The existing level of salary is such that a further salary payment would still suffer NICs at 12%, but the existing income overall is such that income tax is charged at 40%, so this additional salary suffers overall tax at 52%.

62 NINA

(a)   Nina should not have disclosed to anyone any information she acquired through her job.

An AAT student is bound by the principle of confidentiality.

The rules of confidentiality need to be followed even after the client relationship has ended.

(b)   Without the permission of the client, an accountant cannot disclose the error to HMRC as this would be a breach of confidentiality.

However, the accountant has a legal responsibility to report suspicions of money laundering discovered during compliance work to the appointed money laundering officer. Tax evasion is an example of money laundering.

Tutorial note

The duty of confidentiality to the client applies in all circumstances to all individuals, except where there is a legal, regulatory or professional duty to disclose (e.g. suspicion of money laundering). When money laundering is suspected an accountant should report his/her suspicions. This legal duty overrules the duty of confidentiality.

An accountant including an AAT student cannot therefore disclose information, even about a former client, to anyone without the client's permission.

(c)   The type of items in a charity shop can be used by buyers themselves or sold on as part of a trade. However, Franz does not keep them for personal enjoyment, so this indicates trading.

Franz has a profit motive for buying and selling the items, indicating trading.

He has regular transactions and does not keep the items for a long time, which are both badges of trade.

The method of sale, being the use of the online auction site, does not alone indicate trade. However, purchase of a labelling machine indicates Franz is adopting measures to make the process efficient, as would be expected in a trading activity.

Franz is likely to be considered trading.

Tutorial note

Remember to refer to specific badges of trade and the facts of the scenario.

The badges of trade are:

Subject matter (S)

Length of ownership (O)

Frequency of transactions (F)

Improvements or supplementary work (I)

Circumstances of realisation (R)

Profit motive (M)

The following additional badges are also considered:

The source of finance (F)

Method of acquisition (A)

Existence of similar trading transactions (ST)

(d) **Tia's choice of business structure**

Sole trader business

Tia is charged to income tax on the trading profits of the business. The rate of tax is 45% as Tia's other income exceeds £150,000, the higher rate limit.

Tia will pay class 2 national insurance contributions (NICs) of £3.05 per week as her trading profits will exceed £6,515 per annum.

She will pay class 4 NICs on trading profits above £9,568 at 9%.

Company

Corporation tax of 19% is charged on trading profits of £20,000.

Tia could take profits as a dividend. These are not allowable deductions from trading profits so the maximum dividend is the amount after payment of corporation tax. The income tax payable on the dividends would be 38.1%. There is no NIC payable by the company or Mia on the dividend.

Tia could instead be paid a salary by the company. Salaries above a lower limit are charged to employer's NICs at 13.8%. Both the salary and employer's NICs are deductible from trading profits so reduce the company's corporation tax, to nil if the entire profits are withdrawn like this. The salary and employer's NICs together would total £20,000.

The salary would be charged to income tax at 45% and Tia will pay NICs on salary above a lower limit at 12%.

Tutorial note

You may be asked to compare possible business structures. Here the question specified that calculations are not required but you must still consider the amounts in the question to determine appropriate rates of tax. Refer to these in your answer rather than giving general comments.

63 NASHEEN

(a) (i) Nasheen can only discuss Mick's tax affairs with Pamela if the firm has a written letter of authorisation / written permission from Mick.

    (ii) The rules of confidentiality are overridden if there is a legal requirement, or a professional duty or right to disclose information.

Tutorial note

The duty of confidentiality to the client applies in all circumstances to all individuals, except where there is a legal, regulatory or professional duty to disclose (e.g. suspicion of money laundering).

An accountant cannot therefore disclose information to anyone without the client's permission, including the client's spouse or civil partner.

When money laundering is suspected an accountant should report his/her suspicions. This legal duty overrules the duty of confidentiality.

(b) (i) **Profits of the company**

    The profits of the company are charged to corporation tax at 19%

    Dividends

    After deducting the personal allowance of £12,570, dividends falling in the basic rate band (i.e. up to £37,700) are taxed at 7.5%. Dividend income above £50,270 is taxed at 32.5%.

    The maximum dividend paid to Anton is the amount after paying corporation tax, so this will be less than £100,000.

    There are no national insurance contributions paid on dividends.

Salary

By contrast to dividends, the salary is deductible from trading profits and so the full £100,000 can be used. However, employer's NIC is due at 13.8% on salary above a lower limit, and must be paid out of the £100,000 so the gross salary received is less than £100,000.

After deducting the personal allowance of £12,570, salary falling in the basic rate band (i.e. up to £37,700) is taxed at 20% as non-savings income. Salary above £50,270 is taxed at 40%.

Salary above a lower limit is charged to employee's NICs at 12%. Salary above £50,270 is charged at 2%.

(ii)   If Anton had operated as a sole trader, he would have paid income tax on his profits of £100,000. After deducting the personal allowance of £12,570, the rates are 20% for profits falling in the basic rate band (i.e. up to a further £37,700), and 40% for income above £50,270.

Anton would pay class 4 NICs on profits between a lower limit and £50,270 of 9% and 2% above this. He would also pay class 2 NICs of £3.05 per week.

Tutorial note

You may have learned about a dividend nil rate band in other studies. This is not examinable at in this assessment.

64   VICKY

(a)   Vicky has deliberately misled HMRC by providing false information about her trading profits, by failing to include the March 2022 sale. She has reduced her tax liability as a result. This is tax evasion.

It is not tax planning which is use of the law as intended to reduce a tax liability. Vicky could have delayed making the sale until the following year but here the actual sale has taken place already.

It is not tax avoidance which is exploiting the law to reduce tax legally, but in a way not intended by law.

Tutorial note

Tax evasion (such as deliberately failing to disclose all of your income or taking an excessive relief) is illegal.

Tax avoidance uses legal means to reduce your tax bill. Tax avoidance is acting within the law but against the spirit of the law.

Tax planning is using the law as intended to reduce tax, such as taking advantage of reliefs and exemptions.

(b)   An accountant cannot automatically report tax evasion to HMRC as this would be a breach of confidentiality, unless client permission has been given to disclose errors, such as in the engagement letter.

However, the accountant has a duty to report suspicions of money laundering (including tax evasion) to the appointed money laundering officer.

Tutorial note

The duty to report money laundering overrides the principle of confidentiality.

(c)   The initial car was purchased for a hobby for Jason to repair, and then for Jason's own use. This would not appear to be a trading activity.

However, now Jason frequently buys and sells cars and does not keep the cars for long. He also undertakes supplementary work on the cars and has hired premises to carry out the work. He has a profit motive when buying and selling the cars. He finances the purchase of the cars with the profits from the previous cars. These factors indicate that Jason is likely to be considered trading.

Tutorial note

Remember to refer to specific badges of trade and the facts of the scenario.

The badges of trade are:

Subject matter (S)

Length of ownership (O)

Frequency of transactions (F)

Improvements or supplementary work (I)

Circumstances of realisation (R)

Profit motive (M)

The following additional badges are also considered:

The source of finance (F)

Method of acquisition (A)

Existence of similar trading transactions (ST)

(d) Marion currently pays income tax on the dividend income at 32.5% as her other income exceeds the total of the personal allowance and basic rate band.

Marion could give the shares to Geoff so that he receives the dividend income. This would use Geoff's personal allowance and part of his basic rate band taxing only some of the dividends at 7.5%.

The gift of shares between spouses is itself a no gain, no loss (NGNL) transfer for capital gains tax purposes.

In the long term, if the shares are sold, the spouse selling the shares will be assessed on the gain or loss as if he/she has always owned the shares. The effect of this will depend on whether a gain will arise and how much.

If Geoff holds all the shares, he will use first his annual exempt amount and then his basic rate band where the gain is charged to capital gains tax at 10%. Marion may wish to retain some shares to use her annual exempt amount, but not so much that gain is taxed at the higher rate of 20%.

Tutorial note

Married couples or civil partners may be able to hold their investments between them in ways which maximise use of their personal allowances and basic rate bands.

TRADING LOSSES

Key answer tips

The chief assessor has stated in the past that both theory and computational questions on losses seem to cause equal difficulty for learners. This is a surprise, as the expectation would be that computational questions would see a higher level of competence than theory based, but this is not the case. Learners appear to be quite confused over how losses can be relieved and show confusion over the different rules that apply to sole traders and limited companies. Since both might be seen in one task, it is very important to fully understand the rules and the connection between losses carried back, carried forward and relief in the year of the loss.

There is also evidence of learners providing incomplete answers, or simply answering a question as all true or all false, presumably as a quick guess at the answers. Unfortunately this method does not achieve good marks!

65   NICHOLAS

(a)

	True	False
A trading loss made by a company can only be offset against trading profits from the same trade when carrying the loss back		✓
The amount of a trading loss offset against current year profits of a company can be set to preserve the deduction for qualifying charitable donations		✓

Tutorial note

1   *A company has three options for loss relief. It can offset trading losses:*

–   *Against current year total profits only*

–   *Against current year total profits and then carry back against total profits of the previous 12 months (i.e. cannot carry back unless the current year total profits have been relieved)*

–   *Carry the loss forward against total profits.*

2   *Loss relief for a company in the current year or previous 12 months sets the loss against total profits i.e. before qualifying charitable donations, which may then be lost. If the loss is carried forward, the amount of relief set against total profits can be restricted to preserve the use of qualifying charitable donations.*

(b)   **Luka's loss relief options**

Luka can offset the loss against total income in current and/or prior year.

In the current year 2021/22, Luka's only income is savings income of £10,000 so use in the current year would waste the personal allowance and not save tax.

In the prior year 2020/21, Luka has total income of £30,000. Loss relief would use £30,000 of loss (all or nothing claim) but waste the personal allowance. This claim would save income tax at 20% on the income above the personal allowance.

As Luka has ceased to trade, he can claim terminal loss relief. This means the loss is carried back up to three years, and is set against trading profits, with the most recent year first.

The use of the £80,000 loss is therefore:

–   £20,000 in 2020/21, against trading profits some of which would otherwise be covered by the personal allowance, but most of which saves income tax at 20%

–   £35,000 in 2019/20, again wasting some of the personal allowance but mostly saving tax at 20%

–   the remaining loss of £25,000 in 2018/19, all of which saves tax at the basic rate of 20%.

Luka is not able to carry the loss forward against future trading profits as he has ceased to trade.

Recommendation

Therefore Luka should claim terminal loss relief as this uses all the loss and mostly saves tax at 20% while only wasting small amounts of the personal allowance in each year.

Tutorial note

Although the question states that full calculations are not required, you should apply your answer to the scenario in the question. This means using the figures given in the question to work out the rates at which tax would be saved, and whether the personal allowance would be wasted. General comments about loss relief without application to the particular scenario are unlikely to score highly.

For each loss relief option, be careful to specify what the loss can be set against (trading profits only or total income) and in which years. In the case of extended reliefs available when a business starts or ends, be clear to state the order of the relief so in which year the loss is used first.

Remember that the Business Tax reference material gives much of the information needed, but take care to look at the correct column – here for a sole trader, not a company.

The question asked for a recommendation – be sure to give one.

66 JOANNA

(a) Answer = C

Tutorial note

A *There is an option, but no obligation, to offset a sole trader's loss against total income in the current tax year.*

B *A sole trader can offset trading losses against total income in the current tax year and/or prior year in any order. There is no requirement for the preceding year to be relieved first.*

C *Correct answer.*

D *Losses carried forward are set against trading profits only, not total income.*

(b) **Cheny Ltd's loss relief**

Cheny Ltd has ceased to trade, meaning that the loss can be carried back for up to three years against total profits, most recent year first.

Before this, the loss must be used against total profits in the current year (year ended 31 December 2021) of £10,000. The qualifying charitable donations of £20,000 in 2021 are wasted.

The loss is then carried back against the total profits of £170,000 (£160,000 + £10,000) in the year ended 31 December 2020. Again the qualifying charitable donations of £20,000 in 2020 are wasted. Losses remain of £410,000 (£590,000 – £10,000 – £170,000).

In the year ended 31 December 2019, £360,000 (£270,000 + £80,000 + £10,000) is used against total profits, again wasting qualifying charitable donations.

The remaining loss of £50,000 (£410,000 – £360,000) is used against profits in 2018. This leaves profits of £160,000 against which the qualifying charitable donations are set to given taxable total profits of £140,000.

Tutorial note

In a company, the loss is used in the current and previous periods against total profits before qualifying charitable donations meaning these are lost. Total profits include chargeable gains.

The only alternative loss claim would be for the current year only, which would save no tax.

As the company has ceased to trade, the loss cannot be carried forward.

67 STILTON LTD

(a)   The company wants to use the loss as soon as possible so a carry back claim is appropriate.

A current year claim must be made first in the year ended 31 December 2021 to use the loss against the total profits of £600. The qualifying charitable donation of £150 is lost.

The loss is then carried back against the prior year total profits of £10,200. Again, the qualifying charitable donation of £150 is lost.

The remaining loss of £29,200 (£40,000 – £600 – £10,200) is carried forward. The amount of loss claimed to offset against total profits in the year ended 31 December 2022 can be set to preserve the deduction of the qualifying charitable donations. This means £1,950 (£2,100 – £150) is offset and the remaining loss of £27,250 (£29,200 – £1,950) is carried forward to future years.

(b)   The answer is A

Tutorial note

A current year claim must be made before a carry back claim. These claims can lead to the qualifying charitable donations being wasted.

The carried forward loss can be set against total profits, but the amount of loss can be chosen so qualifying charitable donations are not wasted.

68   KANE

(a)

	True	False
A sole trader can offset a trading loss against total income in the current and/or the previous tax year, in any order	✓	
For a trading loss made by a company to be relieved in the preceding accounting period, it must first have been relieved in the current accounting period	✓	
Use of trading loss relief by a company can result in wasted qualifying charitable donations	✓	

(b)   (i)   **Samantha's loss relief to claim relief as early as possible**

To claim relief as early as possible, Samantha should carry back the loss to 2020/21, using £31,000 against her total income (£16,000 + £15,000). This will waste the personal allowance as she cannot claim a lower amount than her total income. The relief will save income tax at the basic rate on income exceeding the personal allowance.

Under Samantha's wishes she will then have a current year claim in 2021/22 of the remaining loss of £7,000 against her total income of £15,000. Most of this is already covered by the personal allowance but income tax at the basic rate will be saved on income exceeding the personal allowance.

(ii)   **Samantha's loss relief to save the most tax**

To save the maximum amount of tax, Samantha could instead carry forward the entire trading loss of £38,000. This will happen automatically if she makes no claims.

Samantha's total income in 2022/23 is expected to be £60,000 (£25,000 + £20,000 + £15,000). She could only use the loss against trading profits of the same trade, meaning £25,000 is used in 2022/23. This would save some tax at the higher rate and some at the basic rate. The personal allowance would not be wasted.

The remaining loss of £13,000 (£38,000 – £25,000) would be carried forward for use against trading profits in future years, which may also save tax at the higher rate.

A disadvantage of this option is that the relief is delayed which means no repayments of tax (or no reduction in payments) for the current/prior years. The trading profits expected may also not arise so there is risk with this option.

Tutorial note

A carried forward loss for a sole trader can only be used against trading profits. This can prolong the loss relief but here gives the opportunity for loss relief at higher rates of tax saving.

The choice of loss relief may be a balance between the amount of tax saved and benefiting earlier with reduced payments or with repayments of tax.

---

69 GREEN LTD

(a) A claim is made to use the brought forward losses against the total profits of the year ended 31 March 2022. The amount is specified to preserve the use of the qualifying charitable donations, so the loss relieved is £215,000 (£175,000 + £30,000 + £20,000 − £10,000).

The remaining trading loss of £15,000 (£230,000 − £215,000) is carried forward for use against total profits in future years.

(b)

	True	False
A sole trader cannot restrict the amount of loss offset in the current year to preserve the personal allowance	✓	
A sole trader can carry forward a loss for a maximum of four years		✓

(c) **Differences between carry forward loss relief in a company and by a sole trader**

The trading loss carried forward in a company is set against total profits. A sole trader can only set carried forward trading losses against trading profits of the same trade.

The loss relief is claimed in a company. For a sole trader, it is automatic for any remaining losses, or if no other claims are made.

The company can choose the amount of loss to relieve up to a maximum of the loss or total profits. The sole trade must use the loss as much as is possible against the first available future trading profits with no restriction.

Tutorial note

Take care when answering a question that you are applying the appropriate rules for that entity and do not confuse the rules for companies and sole traders or partnerships.

The Business Tax reference material can be helpful, showing the different rules in different columns.

70 JOYCE, LIZ AND RON

(a)

	True	False
A trading loss made by a company can only be offset against trading profits from the same trade when carrying the loss forward		✓
The trading loss of a company in the period it ceases to trade can be carried back three years after current year relief	✓	

Tutorial note

A trading loss of a company is carried forward against total profits. A trading loss of a sole trader or partner is carried forward against trading profits of the same trade.

(b) **Partners' loss relief options**

The loss for 2021/22 is £18,000 per partner (£54,000/3).

Joyce

Joyce can make a current year claim against her other income in 2021/22 of £20,000. This would waste most of the personal allowance but save tax at the basic rate on income above the personal allowance.

She could instead make a prior claim against her total income of £32,000 (£20,000 + £24,000/2). There would be no waste of the personal allowance and the entire loss would save tax at the basic rate.

Joyce could instead carry forward the loss against future trading profits from the partnership in 2022/23. Her share is £20,000 (£40,000/2). This would also save tax at the basic rate, and no personal allowance is wasted. However, relief is delayed and relies on the trading profits expected actually being generated.

Therefore, the best option for Joyce is prior year loss relief.

Liz

Liz can also make a current year claim against her other income in 2021/22 of £13,000 but this would mostly just waste the personal allowance and save only a small amount of tax at the basic rate.

She could make a prior year claim against her total income of £25,000 (£13,000 + £24,000/2) which would waste some of the personal allowance and otherwise save tax at the basic rate.

However, as Liz is ceasing to trade by retiring, she can claim terminal loss relief. She can carry the loss back against trading profits for up to three years, most recent year first. This means using £12,000 of the loss against trading profits of 2020/21. There is no loss of the personal allowance and the saving is all at the basic rate.

The remaining £6,000 is carried back to 2019/20 and used against Liz's share of the partnership trading profit of £15,000 (£30,000/2). This saves tax at the basic rate and wastes none of the personal allowance given Liz's other income.

Liz cannot carry the loss forward to use against future trading profits from the partnership as she is no longer trading.

The best option for Liz is to claim terminal loss relief.

Ron

Ron has no other income in 2021/22 or in 2020/21 and so cannot make a current year or prior year claim.

He could carry the loss of £18,000 forward against his share of the partnership trading profit of £20,000 in 2022/23. As he has no other income, this would waste most of the personal allowance and otherwise save tax at the basic rate on income above the personal allowance.

However, Ron joined the partnership in 2021/22 and so the loss arises in one of his first four years of trade. He can claim opening years loss relief and carry the loss back against total income of the previous three years, earliest year first.

This means setting the £18,000 loss against his total income of £30,000 in 2018/19. Most of this saves tax at the basic rate with a small amount of waste of the personal allowance. Ron will receive a repayment.

The best option for Ron is to use opening years relief to save tax as quickly and as much as possible.

Tutorial note

The loss relief options for partners are considered separately. Watch out for partners joining the partnership who qualify for opening years relief, and for partners leaving where terminal loss relief may be the best option.

The question asked for a recommendation – be sure to give one.

71 DONAL

(a) **Donal's loss relief options**

Donal can claim relief for the loss of £45,000 against his current year income of £60,000 in 2021/22. This will save some income tax at the higher rate but most at the basic rate.

The same result would be achieved if Donal were to claim loss relief in the prior year.

As this is a trading loss of one of the first four years of trade, Donal can claim opening years relief against total income in the three previous years, earliest year first. That means Donal can claim relief against his income of £200,000 in 2018/19. This saves income tax at the additional rate and Donal will receive a repayment.

Donal could carry the loss forward to future years to offset against his future trading income. This would save tax at the higher rate, but relies on trading profits being generated. With current predictions this will take more one year in future to relieve the loss.

The best option for Donal is opening years relief as this gives the highest tax saving as soon as possible.

Tutorial note

The information in the question may not be provided in summary tables, and you should spend some time making sure you understand which income arises in which years. Only then will you be able to work out the optimum loss relief.

The question asked for a recommendation – be sure to give one.

(b) **Use of Brick Ltd's trading loss**

The company wants to use the loss as soon as possible.

Before making a carry back claim, Brick Ltd must make a current year claim against total profits before qualifying charitable donations of £24,000 in the year ended 30 September 2020. Qualifying charitable donations in this year are lost.

The loss can then be carried back against the total profits before qualifying charitable donations of £224,000 (£200,000 + 24,000) in the year ended 30 September 2019. Qualifying charitable donations in this year are lost.

The remaining loss is £152,000 (£400,000 – £24,000 – £224,000). This is carried forward against the total profits of the year ended 30 September 2022, but the amount can be set to preserve the charitable donations of £15,000. So the loss relieved is £141,000 (£100,000 + £56,000 – £15,000). The remaining loss of £11,000 is carried forward.

Tutorial note

The company is in its early years of trading but there is no equivalent of opening years loss relief for companies. Special loss relief for early years exists only for sole traders and partnerships.

BUSINESS DISPOSALS

72   SUSAN AND RACHEL

(a)   The answer is C

Tutorial note

Business asset disposal relief is available as Susan has made a qualifying disposal and she has owned the business for at least two years.

The annual exempt amount is deducted from the antique table gain first, leaving all of the business gain to be charged to tax. The business gain is then taxed at 10% as business asset disposal relief is available.

The business gain must be taxed first, before the antique table gain, to use up any remaining basic rate band (if applicable).

The antique table gain, after the annual exempt amount, is therefore taxed at 20% as Susan is a higher rate taxpayer.

(b)   **Gain/loss on disposal**

Asset	Capital gain/(loss)
	£
Workshop	85,000
Plant	0
Inventory	0
Goodwill	175,000

Workings

Workshop gain = (£200,000 – £115,000) = £85,000

Goodwill gain = (£175,000 – £0) = £175,000

Tutorial note

An allowable capital loss does not arise on the sale of the plant because the plant qualifies for capital allowances.

Inventory is not a capital asset. Sale of inventory gives rise to a trading profit or loss.

(c)

	True	False
Gift relief is available on a gain on the gift of shares in a quoted investment company provided the donor owned at least 5% of the shares		✓
The gain on a gift of any holding of shares in an unquoted trading company qualifies for gift relief	✓	
Gift relief defers the gain on a gift of a qualifying asset until the recipient sells the asset	✓	
A gain on the gift of an asset used in the trade of the donor does not qualify for gift relief if the donor has not owned the asset for at least two years		✓

Tutorial note

Gift relief is not available on a gain on investment company shares. The company must be a trading company. If the trading company is quoted, it must be the donor's personal company (5% shareholding required).

The asset does not have to be held for a particular time period, but it does have to be used in the trade of the donor or that of the donor's personal trading company.

73 NORMAN

(a) Norman's capital gains tax payable in 2021/22 is £68,770

Working

	£
Chargeable gain on the shares	700,000
Less: Annual exempt amount	(12,300)
Taxable gain	687,700
Capital gains tax at 10%	68,770

Tutorial note

Business asset disposal relief will apply here which means the gain will be taxed at 10%. Norman's shareholding represents a greater than 5% interest in the company and has been working for the company. In addition, he satisfies both of these conditions for the most recent 24 months.

(b)   31 January 2024

(i.e. 12 months from 31 January following the end of the tax year in which the disposal occurred)

(c)   **Tax effect of disposals**

Asset	Tax effect
Storage garage	capital gain
Computer equipment	trading profit increase
Inventory	trading profit increase
Goodwill	capital gain

Tutorial note

The workshop and goodwill are capital assets sold for more than cost and so a capital gain arises in each chase.

The computer equipment is a capital asset but it is eligible for capital allowances and so a capital loss does not arise on its disposal. However, the proceeds are deducted from the general pool leading to a balancing charge of £3,000 which increases the trading profits.

The inventory is not capital, and sale for more than cost gives rise to an increase in trading profits.

(d) (i)   Dinah's taxable gain for 2021/22 is £2,275,400

 (ii)   Dinah's capital gains tax payable for 2021/22 is £355,080

 (iii)   Her net proceeds after tax are £1,942,620

Working

	£
Net proceeds (£2,300,000 – £2,300)	2,297,700
Less: Cost	(10,000)
Chargeable gain	2,287,700
Less: Annual exempt amount	(12,300)
Taxable gain	2,275,400
Capital gains tax £1,000,000 × 10%	100,000
Capital gains tax £1,275,400 × 20%	255,080
Total capital gains tax	355,080

	£
Net proceeds (£2,300,000 – £2,300)	2,297,700
Less: total capital gains tax	(355,080)
Net proceeds after tax	1,942,620

Tutorial note

Remember that the taxable gain is after deduction of the annual exempt amount. The legal fees on sale are allowable deductions when calculating the gain.

Dinah has sold a trading company, in which she owned at least 5% of the shares, and where she was an employee, and these conditions have been met for at least two years. Business asset disposal relief (BADR) is available.

There is a lifetime limit of £1,000,000 for BADR. This amount of the taxable gain is charged at 10% and the excess is charged at 20%.

You may be asked to calculate 'after tax proceeds', 'post tax proceeds' or 'net proceeds after tax'. These terms all mean the same thing. The capital gains tax on the disposal should be deducted from the proceeds. Costs of sale may be deducted, but not the original cost of the shares. A common mistake is to deduct the tax from the gains figure.

74 HARRY AND BRIONY

(a) Harry's capital gains tax payable is £1,027,540.

Working: Capital gains tax – 2021/22

	£
Chargeable gain	5,500,000
Less: Annual exempt amount	(12,300)
Taxable gain	5,487,700
Gains qualifying for business asset disposal relief (£1,000,000 lifetime allowance – £300,000 used in 2020/21)	
= £700,000 × 10%	70,000
Remaining gain (£5,487,700 – £700,000) = £4,787,700 × 20%	957,540
	1,027,540

(b) The answer is C – gift relief is only available to individuals

(c) (i) Briony's taxable gain for 2021/22 is £372,700

    (ii) Briony's capital gains tax payable for 2021/22 is £37,270

    (iii) Her post tax proceeds are £752,730

Working

	£
Gain on office building	125,000
Gain on goodwill	260,000
Chargeable gains on business disposal	385,000
Less: Annual exempt amount	(12,300)
Taxable gain	372,700
Capital gains tax at 10%	37,270

	£
Proceeds	790,000
Less: Capital gains tax	(37,270)
Net proceeds after tax	752,730

(d)   (i)   Ranj could sell his business on 31 December 2021.

Tutorial note

The business must be owned for at least 24 months ending with the date of disposal to qualify for business asset disposal relief.

If you answered 1 January 2022, you should still be given credit.

   (ii)   Ranj must make a claim for business asset disposal relief by 31 January 2024.

75   CHERYL

(a)   The answer is A

Tutorial note

The business asset disposal relief (BADR) limit of £1,000,000 is a lifetime limit.

BADR is available to individuals only on the sale of whole or part of a business or certain disposals of shares. It is not available on the sale of individual assets of a business.

(b)

	True	False
If the tax written down value on the general pool exceeds the disposal value of plant, a balancing allowance arises	✓	
The sale of goodwill which has been generated by Gio may give rise to a capital loss		✓
If Gio had traded for 13 months, business asset disposal relief would not be available	✓	
An allowable capital loss may arise on the sale of the plant used in the business		✓

Tutorial note

When a trader disposes of his business he/she ceases to trade. There are balancing adjustments on the disposal of plant. If the TWDV is greater than the disposal value, a balancing allowance arises. If the proceeds of the disposed plant exceeds TWDV, a balancing charge arises.

Goodwill generated by the trader (rather than purchased) has nil cost. If any proceeds of the business disposal relate to goodwill, a gain will arise but not a loss.

An allowable capital loss does not arise if plant is sold for less than cost as the plant was eligible for capital allowances in the business.

(c) (i) The gift relief claimed is £290,000

(ii) Aljaz's taxable gain if gift relief is not claimed is £277,700

(iii) Aljaz's capital gains tax payable for 2021/22 is £50,540

Working

	£
Proceeds	350,000
Less: cost	(60,000)
Chargeable gain	290,000
Less: Annual exempt amount	(12,300)
Taxable gain	277,700
Capital gains tax £50,000 (£1,000,000 – £950,000) × 10%	5,000
Capital gains tax £227,700 × 20%	45,540
Total capital gains tax	50,540

Tutorial note

If gift relief is claimed, this reduces the gain (before annual exempt amount) to nil.

If business asset disposal relief is claimed instead, this reduces the capital gains tax rate, but not the gain. There is a lifetime limit of £1,000,000 and so only £50,000 of the gain on disposal qualifies for business asset disposal relief. The remaining gain is taxed at 20%.

76   RALF

(a)   **Tax effect of disposals**

Asset	Tax effect
Goodwill	capital gain
Warehouse	capital loss
Machinery	trading profit decrease
Inventory	trading profit decrease

Tutorial note

The goodwill and warehouse are capital assets, but the warehouse is sold for less than cost so a capital loss arises.

The machinery is a capital asset but it is eligible for capital allowances and so a capital loss does not arise on its disposal. However, the machinery is removed from the general pool. There is no proceeds so the disposal value is nil, and a balancing allowance arises equal to the TWDV. This decreases the trading profits.

The inventory is not capital, and sale for less than cost decreases the trading profits.

(b)   (i)   Taylor's taxable gain for 2021/22 is £396,700

(ii)   Taylor's capital gains tax payable for 2021/22 is £79,340

(iii)   Her net proceeds after tax are £330,660

Working

	£
Proceeds	410,000
Less: Cost	(1,000)
Chargeable gain	409,000
Less: Annual exempt amount	(12,300)
Taxable gain	396,700
Capital gains tax £396,700 × 20%	79,340

	£
Proceeds	410,000
Less: Capital gains tax	(79,340)
Net proceeds after tax	330,660

Tutorial note

Taylor has sold a trading company, in which she owned at least 5% of the shares, and where she was an employee, and these conditions have been met for at least two years. Business asset disposal relief (BADR) should be available.

However, there is a lifetime limit of £1,000,000 for BADR and this will have been fully used by the disposal in 2018/19. The taxable gain is charged at 20%.

Remember not to deduct the original cost of the shares when calculating the net proceeds after tax.

(c)

	True	False
Gift relief is available on a gain on the gift of unquoted trading company shares, regardless of the size of the shareholding	✓	
If a sole trader sells a building but continues to trade, business asset disposal relief is not available	✓	
Business asset disposal relief applies automatically on a disposal of a business if the gain does not exceed £1,000,000		✓
Business asset disposal relief defers a gain on disposal of unquoted trading company shares until the recipient sells the shares		✓

Tutorial note

Business asset disposal relief is only available when the whole or part of a business is sold, not on the sale of individual assets.

Business asset disposal relief must be claimed and the £1,000,000 is a lifetime limit on all qualifying disposals.

Gift relief defers a gain. Business asset disposal relief reduces the rate of capital gains tax to 10% on gains up to the lifetime limit.

77 STEPHAN

(a) **Gain/loss on disposal**

Asset	Capital gain/(loss)
	£
Goodwill	80,000
Industrial building	320,000
Plant	0
Inventory	0

Workings

Gain on goodwill = (£80,000 − £0) = £80,000

Gain on industrial building = (£870,000 − £550,000) = £320,000

Tutorial note

The proceeds are deemed to be the market values of the assets.

An allowable capital loss does not arise on the sale of the plant because the plant qualifies for capital allowances.

(b) (i) Sajid's taxable gain for 2021/22 is £57,700

(ii) Sajid's capital gains tax payable for 2021/22 is £5,770

(iii) His post tax proceeds are £764,230

Working

	£
Gain on goodwill	100,000
Loss on factory	(30,000)
Chargeable gains on business disposal	70,000
Less: Annual exempt amount	(12,300)
Taxable gain	57,700
Capital gains tax at 10%	5,770

	£
Proceeds (£100,000 + £600,000 + £50,000 + £20,000)	770,000
Less: Capital gains tax	(5,770)
Net proceeds after tax	764,230

Tutorial note

There is no need to calculate Sajid's unused basic rate band, as the gains qualify for business asset disposal relief and will be taxed at 10% regardless of which tax band they fall into.

(c)

	True	False
If a sole trader gifts an asset used in the trade but continues to trade, gift relief is not available		✓
Business asset disposal relief reduces the rate of capital gains tax on the gain on the sale of a business	✓	
To qualify for business asset disposal relief on the sale of a business, the trader must have operated the business for at least two years	✓	
There is a lifetime limit of £1,000,000 on gains qualifying for gift relief		✓

Tutorial note

Gift relief is available on the gift of a single asset used in the donor's trade. Business asset disposal relief would not be available on disposal of a single asset.

The lifetime limit of £1,000,000 applies to business asset disposal relief and not gift relief.

78   LEIGH

(a)   **Gain/loss on disposal**

Asset	Capital gain/(loss)
	£
Goodwill	50,000
Storage unit	55,000
Plant	0

Workings

Gain on goodwill = (£50,000 – £0) = £50,000

Gain on storage unit = (£80,000 – £25,000) = £55,000

Tutorial note

An allowable capital loss does not arise on the sale of the plant because the plant qualifies for capital allowances.

(b)

	True	False
A trader who ceases to trade after two years, and sells the assets of the business for a gain within four years of the cessation can claim business asset disposal relief		✓
To claim gift relief on the disposal of unquoted trading company shares, the donor must have worked for the company for two years		✓
Gift relief is available if quoted trading company shares are gifted, provided the donor had a shareholding of at least 5%	✓	
If the proceeds on the sale of a business exceed £1,000,000, business asset disposal relief is always only partially available		✓

Tutorial note

*Following a cessation of trade, the business assets must be sold within **three** years for business asset disposal relief to be available. It is correct that the trader must have traded for at least two years.*

There is no requirement for the donor to work for the company to qualifying for gift relief on the disposal of unquoted trading company shares. This is a requirement for business asset disposal relief.

The business asset disposal relief lifetime limit of £1,000,000 applies to the gain, and not the level of proceeds.

(c)   **Capital gains tax reliefs**

Disposal	Capital gains tax relief(s)
Gift of a building used in the continuing trade of a sole trader	gift relief
Sale of shares in an unquoted investment company, wholly owned by the seller, where the seller has worked for 20 years	neither business asset disposal relief nor gift relief
Gift of a sole trader business which has operated for ten years	business asset disposal relief and gift relief
Gift of shares in a quoted trading company where the donor has held 6% of the shares for five years but did not work for the company	gift relief
Sale of an interest in a partnership by a partner who joined five years earlier	business asset disposal relief

Tutorial note

Business asset disposal relief is not available on the gift of a single asset from an ongoing business.

For both reliefs, the company must be a trading company, not an investment company.

There is no requirement for the donor to work for the company to qualifying for gift relief on the disposal of trading company shares. This is a requirement for business asset disposal relief. If the shares are in a quoted company, the donor must own at least 5%.

Business asset disposal relief is available on a disposal of an interest in a partnership.

Section 3

MOCK ASSESSMENT QUESTIONS

TASK 1 **(8 marks)**

This task is about adjusting accounting profits and losses for tax purposes.

Safari Ltd, a UK company, has the following statement of profit or loss for the year ended 30 June 2021:

	£	£
Revenue		350,569
Less: Cost of sales		(195,053)
		———
Gross profit		155,516
Wages and salaries	34,734	
Travelling and entertaining	2,357	
Motor expenses	2,814	
Legal and professional fees	1,830	
Depreciation	3,656	
Other general expenses	1,225	
	———	(46,616)
		———
Net profit		108,900
		———

The following further information is given:

1 **Travelling and entertaining expenses**

These include expenses of entertaining UK customers of £391 and gifts to customers of bottles of champagne costing £634 (cost approximately £45 each).

2 **Legal and professional fees**

The figure in the accounts is can be broken down as follows:

	£
Legal fees in connection with new office purchase	390
Payment to customer for breach of contract	1,440

3 **Other general expenses**

These include a donation of £240 to the Labour Party.

Calculate the tax adjusted trading profit for Safari Ltd by entering adjustments to accounting profit below. If no adjustment is required, you should enter a 0 (zero). If any adjustments are deducted from accounting profits, these should be shown as a negative figure (for example, a deduction of 5,000 should be shown as -5000 or -5,000) **(8 marks)**

	£
Net profit	108,900
Wages and salaries	
Entertaining UK customers	
Gifts to customers	
Motor expenses	
Legal fees in connection with new office purchase	
Payment to customer for breach of contract	
Depreciation	
Labour Party donation	
Tax adjusted trading profit	

TASK 2 (12 marks)

This task is about capital allowances.

Scharrett Ltd has the following non-current asset information for the seven month period ended 31 July 2021:

	£
Balances brought forward as at 1 January 2021:	
General pool	14,000
Special rate pool	16,000
Additions in January 2021:	
Plant	590,250
Additions in May 2021:	
New machinery	201,500
Finance Director's car (new Nissan) (40% private use)	15,000
Managing Director's car (Audi) (75% private use)	32,000
Disposals in June 2021:	
Machinery (cost £11,000)	10,100
Managing Director's car (Renault) (cost £17,200)	13,600

The cars have CO_2 emissions as follows:

Nissan	0g/km
Audi	46g/km
Renault	105g/km

(a) Complete the capital allowance computation for the period ended 31 July 2021. The brought forward figures have already been entered.

You should ensure that:

– any additions qualifying for AIA, FYA or the super deduction are included in the appropriate column

– all allowances are included in the total allowances column

– the total allowances for the period are clearly shown

– carried forward balances are clearly shown.

Any columns that are not required should be left blank. (9 marks)

	AIA	FYA	Super deduction	General pool	Special rate pool	Private use asset	Allowances
	£	£	£	£	£	£	£
TWDV b/f				14,000	16,000		

(b) **Identify whether the following statements relating to the structures and buildings allowance are true or false.** **(3 marks)**

	True	False
Land originally acquired to construct the building 9 months before construction started can be included in the structures and building allowance calculation		
Structures and building allowance is claimed from the date the building is brought into use		
Structures and buildings allowance is not time apportioned for a short accounting period, it is given in full		

TASK 3 (6 marks)

This task is about basis period rules.

Kenza started trading on 1 January 2018. She prepared her first set of accounts to 31 May 2018 and then to 31 May each year.

The adjusted profits were as follows:

	£
Period ended 31 May 2018	19,040
Year ended 31 May 2019	43,200

(a) **(i)** **In which tax year did Kenza start trading?** (1 mark)

    A   2016/17

    B   2017/18

    C   2018/19

    D   2019/20

    (ii) **What are Kenza's taxable trading profits for the first tax year of trading?** (1 mark)

    A   £19,040

    B   £15,232

    C   £7,616

    D   £11,424

    (iii) **What are Kenza's taxable trading profits for the second tax year of trading?** (1 mark)

    A   £43,200

    B   £19,040

    C   £44,240

    D   £40,640

    (iv) **What are Kenza's overlap profits? State your answer to the nearest pound.** (1 mark)

£

    (v) **Identify whether the following statements are true or false.** (2 marks)

	True	False
If Kenza has a loss in the final period of trade, she cannot deduct overlap profits from it to calculate her final period's results		
Kenza could not have chosen a period longer than 12 months as her accounting period		

TASK 4 (8 marks)

This task is about analysing profits and losses of a partnership and calculating NICs.

Mary and Fred have traded in partnership for many years as bakers and have the following profit share arrangement:

- Each partner has an annual salary of £30,000 (£15,000 until 1 October 2021)

- The partners shared profits in the ratio 2:3 until 1 October 2021 when they changed it to 1:1

- Mary has a return on capital of 5%. Her capital invested is £15,000

The partnership's tax adjusted trading profits for the year ended 31 January 2022 are £189,600.

(a) **Calculate the trading profit for each partner by completing the appropriation of profits statement below. State your answer to the nearest pound.** (6 marks)

	Mary	Fred	Total
	£	£	£
Period to 30 September 2021			
Salary	10,000	10,000	20,000
Interest on capital	500	0	500
Profit share			
Total			
Period to 31 January 2022			
Salary			
Interest on capital			
Profit share			
Total			
Total for the year			

Ting has taxable trading profits of £53,000 for 2021/22.

(b) **Calculate the total amount of class 4 NICs payable by Ting (to the nearest penny).**

(2 marks)

£ [   ]

TASK 5 (6 marks)

This task is about chargeable gains and allowable losses of companies.

Walkden Ltd disposed of an item of plant in the year ended 31 March 2021 for sales proceeds of £126,000. Walkden Ltd had to pay legal fees of £450 on the sale.

The plant cost £46,000 in October 2011, plus legal fees of £1,200 to facilitate the purchase. In January 2015, Walkden Ltd decided to upgrade the plant to improve its output at a cost of £4,500. In December 2019, the plant broke down and had to be repaired at a cost of £250.

The relevant indexation factors are detailed below:

October 2011 to December 2017 = 0.168

January 2015 to December 2017 = 0.089

(a) **Calculate the chargeable gain to be included in the corporation tax computation of Walkden Ltd for the year ended 31 March 2021. Any amounts to be deducted in calculating the gain should be shown as a negative figure (for example, a deduction of 5,000 should be shown as -5000 or -5,000). All entries should be stated to the nearest pound.** (5 marks)

	£
Proceeds	
Selling expenses	
Cost including acquisition expenses	
Enhancement expenditure	
Indexation allowance	
Gain	

(b) **Identify which ONE of the following statements is true:** (1 mark)

Any asset purchased by a company qualifies for rollover relief	
The amount of rollover relief claimed is deducted from the gain on the disposal of the new asset	
When making a claim for rollover relief, a company can choose the amount of gain to be rolled over	
For rollover relief to be available, the purchase of the new asset must be between 1 year before and 3 years after the disposal of the old asset	

TASK 6 (9 marks)

This task is about calculating chargeable gains and allowable losses in company disposal of shares.

Pageant plc bought 1,500 shares in Calcot Ltd for £14,500 on 15 July 2012.

A bonus issue of 1 for 6 shares was made on 7 May 2013.

On 31 October 2021 the company bought 400 shares for £15.50 per share.

On 5 November 2021, the company sold 750 shares for £16.80 per share.

Indexation factors were:

July 2012 to May 2013	0.033
May 2013 to December 2017	0.112
July 2012 to December 2017	0.149

(a) Complete the share pool for Pageant plc. Show the balance of shares carried forward. Show your answers to the nearest pound. You have been given more space than you will need.

(5 marks)

Description	Number of shares	Cost £	Indexed cost £
15 July 2012 - purchase	1,500	14,500	14,500

(b) Calculate the chargeable gain or allowable loss on the disposal of the 750 shares in Pageant plc. Show your answer to the nearest pound.

(4 marks)

	£

TASK 7 (6 marks)

This task is about calculating taxable profits and corporation tax payable.

In the 16-month period ended 31 January 2022, Deckchair Ltd had the following results:

Trading profits	£864,000
Chargeable gain – 8 August 2021	£319,000
Interest received	£16,320
Donation to charity – 1 March 2021	£4,000

Calculate the taxable profits for each period by completing the table below. Any amounts decreasing taxable profits should be shown with a negative figure (for example, a deduction of 5,000 should be shown as -5000 or -5,000). (6 marks)

State all answers to the nearest pound. Leave blank any boxes where no entry is required.

	First period £	Second period £
Trading profit		
Investment income		
Chargeable gains		
Qualifying charitable donations		
Taxable profits		

TASK 8   **(15 marks)**

This task is about the administrative requirements for UK tax law.

(a)   (i)   **What is the deadline for the payment of corporation tax for a single company with the year end 31 August 2021 that has augmented profits below £1,500,000?**

(1 mark)

[   ]

     (ii)   **By when must a company with the year ended 31 May 2021 submit its corporation tax return?**   **(1 mark)**

[   ]

     (iii)   **What is the last instalment payment date for a large company with a 31 March 2022 year end?**

(1 mark)

[   ]

(b)   **Dominic asks whether the following statements are true or false.**

Tick the appropriate box for each statement.   **(3 marks)**

	True	False
The maximum penalty for mistakes in a tax return due to carelessness is 50%		
A company with a period of account ending 30 September 2021 must pay a penalty of £3,000 if it does not retain its records until 30 September 2027		
There are no circumstances in which client confidentiality can be breached		

Micah started trading on 1 October 2021.

(c)   (i)   **What are the correct deadlines for Micah for the actions below:**   **(3 marks)**

You should state the dates in full.

Action	Deadline
Notify HMRC of chargeability	
File a tax return online for the first tax year of trade	
File a paper return for the first tax year of trade	

Assume that Micah filed his 2021/22 tax return on 15 October 2023 and paid his liability of £800 on the same day.

     (ii)   **Calculate the penalty amounts that Micah will have to pay as a result of his late filing.**

(3 marks)

Penalty	£
Fixed	
Daily	
Tax-geared penalty	

(iii) **Complete the following sentence by filling in the blanks, using the options below. Each option may only be used once:** (2 marks)

Micah must keep records for _____ years, from _____

1	the end of his first month of trading
3	the end of the tax year
5	the filing date for the tax year
10	the first day of trading

(iv) **From the options below, select which tax Micah will NOT have to pay as a sole trader:** (1 mark)

Income tax	
Class 1 primary NICs	
Class 1 secondary NICs	
Class 4 NICs	

TASK 9 (12 marks)

This task is about tax planning and the responsibilities of the business and agent.

Lubna has been trading for a few years selling small jewellery items. If her family members buy her items, she charges them full price but asks them to pay cash so that she doesn't have to include the sales in her accounts or tax return.

(a) **(i)** **Define tax evasion and tax avoidance.** (2 marks)

(ii) **Identify whether Lubna is engaging in tax evasion, tax avoidance, or tax planning.**
(1 mark)

Ju was always struggling to find her house keys in her handbag and decided to make herself a keyring with a hook attached, so that she could fasten it to a loop in her bag, making the keys easier to find and more secure.

Her family and friends thought the idea was great, so she made a few more keyrings and gave them to them for free as gifts. Since then, the keyrings have gained popularity and so Ju has started selling them to many others at a profit. Ju has asked her customers to put photos of their keyrings online if they like them. Ju has also started posting photos of the keyrings online, to try to increase interest in them.

(b) **(i)** **Discuss whether Ju is trading by reference to the badges of trade. You do not need to make a conclusion.** (3 marks)

Assume Ju decides to set up her keyring business formally and anticipates being profitable in the first few years. She is unsure whether to set up the business as an unincorporated business or as a limited company. Regardless of the structure, she intends to draw a salary out of the business.

(ii)   Explain the tax implications of each business structure that Ju is considering, identifying which types of tax will be due and at what rates. You are not required to complete tax computations or do any detailed calculations.   (6 marks)

TASK 10 (8 marks)

This task is about trading losses.

Angelique set up a business on 1 April 2021 selling homemade cakes and cupcakes. Prior to that, Angelique's only other source of income was from renting out some investment properties, which earned her around £34,000 per year. Angelique continues to rent the properties out, alongside running her new business.

During her first period, Angelique has incurred large costs in setting up her business, including expenditure on new equipment to make, bake and decorate the cakes. As a result, she has made a trading loss of £78,000. In future years she expects to make trading profits of around £25,000 per year.

(a) **Explain the loss options available to Angelique and recommend the most appropriate option for her to use** **(5 marks)**

You do not have to show detailed calculations, but may use numbers to support your answer

Green Ltd has been trading for many years. In the year ended 31 March 2022, the company had a large warehouse fire, which halted production for 3 months of the year and resulted in significant costs being incurred as the company did not have insurance. As a result, the company made a loss, but production and sales are expected to slowly return back to their original level in the next few years.

Information about the company's results for the last few years are as follows:

	Year ended 31 March 2021	Year ended 31 March 2022	Year ended 31 March 2023
	£	£	£
Trading profit/(loss)	570,000	(894,000)	129,000
Investment income	42,000	23,000	34,000
QCDs	7,000	2,000	5,000

Green Ltd wants loss relief as early as possible.

(b) Explain how Green Ltd can maximise its loss relief. Identify how much loss relief will be utilised in each relevant year. **(3 marks)**

TASK 11 (10 marks)

This task is about business disposals.

Amandeep has run his unquoted sole trader business for many years and after a decline in sales over the last few years, he has decided to sell his business on 31 May 2021.

On 31 May 2021, Amandeep had the following assets:

	Market value at cessation £	Original cost £	Tax written down value £
Warehouse	260,000	195,000	
Machinery	50,000	75,000	37,000
Goodwill	380,000	0	

(a) (i) Identify any capital gain or loss that may arise on the disposal of each asset assuming no reliefs are claimed. If no gain or loss arises, enter 0 (zero). Any loss should be shown as a negative number. (3 marks)

	Capital gain/loss £
Warehouse	
Machinery	
Goodwill	

(ii) Amandeep wasn't sure whether to gift the business outright to his son, or sell it to a third party. Identify whether the each of the following statements are true or false. (4 marks)

	True	False
Gift relief is only available if an individual gives qualifying assets to family members		
Assets used in the trade of a sole trader are qualifying assets for gift relief		
Gift relief applies automatically to a qualifying disposal		
Business asset disposal relief is only available if Amandeep sells his business to a third party		

Stacey purchased 1,000 £1 shares (a 25% holding) in Brew Ltd (a trading company) at par many years ago when she stated working for the company. She sold the shares for £270,000 on 1February 2022.

Stacey made no other disposals during the tax year 2021/22 and is a higher rate taxpayer.

(b) **(i)** **Calculate Stacey's taxable gain on the disposal of the shares. State your answer to the nearest pound.** **(1 mark)**

£

(ii) **Calculate the capital gains tax payable by Stacey, assuming all beneficial reliefs are claimed. State your answer to the nearest pound.** **(1 mark)**

£

(iii) **Calculate Stacey's proceeds after tax from the disposal of the shares. State your answer to the nearest pound.** **(1 mark)**

£

Section 4

MOCK ASSESSMENT ANSWERS

TASK 1

Safari Ltd – tax adjusted trading profit – year ended 30 June 2021

	£
Net profit	108,900
Wages and salaries	0
Entertaining UK customers	391
Gifts to customers	634
Motor expenses	0
Legal fees in connection with new office purchase	390
Payment to customer for breach of contract	0
Depreciation	3,656
Labour Party donation	240
Tax adjusted trading profit	114,211

Tutorial note

1   *Depreciation and the legal fees in relation to the new office are all capital in nature and must be added back.*

2   *Entertaining is not an allowable deduction, unless it is in respect of entertaining staff.*

3   *Gifts to customers costing less than £50 per person per year and carrying a conspicuous advertisement for the business are tax allowable, unless they are gifts of food, drink, tobacco or vouchers. Although the bottles of champagne cost less than £50 each, the cost is disallowed as the gift is of drink.*

4   *Donations to political parties are not allowable deductions.*

TASK 2

(a)   **Scharrett Ltd – Capital allowances computation – seven months ended 31 July 2021**

	AIA	FYA	Super deduction	General pool	Special rate pool	Private use asset	Allowances
TWDV b/f				14,000	16,000		
Additions:							
Nissan car		15,000					
FYA		(15,000)					15,000
Audi car				32,000			
Plant	590,250						
AIA	(583,333)						583,333
				6,917			
Machinery			201,500				
Super deduction			(201,500)				261,950
Disposals:							
Machinery				(10,100)			
Renault car					(13,600)		
				42,817	2,400		
WDA 18% × 7/12				(4,496)			4,496
WDA 6% × 7/12					(84)		84
TWDV c/f				38,321	2,316		
Total							864,863

Working

The maximum AIA for the seven months ended 31 July 2021 is £583,333 (£1,000,000 × 7/12).

Tutorial note

1   *Private use of assets by an employee is irrelevant in a capital allowances computation; the allowances are available in full. The individual is assessed on the private use element in his/her personal income tax computation as an employment benefit.*

2   *Capital allowances on car purchases are calculated based on the CO_2 emissions of the car as follows:*

—   new car with zero CO_2 emissions:

eligible for a FYA of 100% (i.e. the Nissan)

— CO_2 emissions of between 1 – 50g/km:

put in main pool and eligible for a WDA at 18% (i.e. the Audi)

— CO_2 emissions of > 50g/km:

put in special rate pool (i.e. the Renault) and eligible for a WDA at 6%.

3   *Qualifying plant and machinery purchased after 1 April 2021 is eligible for the 130% super deduction. Plant and machinery purchased before this date is entitled to AIA, with no super deduction.*

3   *Disposals are deducted at the lower of cost and sale proceeds.*

4   *The accounting period is seven months in length, therefore the AIA and the WDA must be time apportioned by 7/12. However, the FYA is never time apportioned.*

(b)

	True	False
Land originally acquired to construct the building 9 months before construction started can be included in the structures and building allowance calculation		✓
Structures and building allowance is claimed from the date the building is brought into use	✓	
Structures and buildings allowance is not time apportioned for a short accounting period, it is given in full		✓

TASK 3

Kenza

(a)   (i)   B

(ii)   D

(iii)   C

(iv)   £36,624

Working

Tax year	Basis period	Assessment £
2017/18	Actual basis 1 January 2018 – 5 April 2018 (3/5 × £19,040)	11,424
2018/19	Actual basis 1 January 2018 – 31 December 2018 (5/5 × 19,040 +7/12 × £43,200)	44,240
2019/20	Current year basis year ended 31 May 2019	43,200
Overlap profits	1 January 2018 – 5 April 2018 (3/5 × £19,040) 1 June 2018 – 31 December 2018 (7/12 × £43,200)	36,624

(v)

	True	False
If Kenza has a loss in the final period of trade, she cannot deduct overlap profits from it to calculate her final period's results		✓
Kenza could not have chosen a period longer than 12 months as her accounting period		✓

TASK 4

(a)

	Mary	Fred	Total
	£	£	£
Period to 30 September 2021 (8 months)			
Salary	10,000	10,000	20,000
Interest on capital	500	0	500
Profit share (2:3)	42,360	63,540	105,900
Total (8 months)	52,860	73,540	126,400
Period to 31 January 2022 (4 months)			
Salary (4/12 × £30,000)	10,000	10,000	20,000
Interest on capital (4/12 × £15,000 × 5%))	250	0	250
Profit share (1:1)	21,475	21,475	42,950
Total (4 months)	31,725	31,475	63,200
Total for the year	**84,585**	**105,015**	**189,600**

(b)   **Class 4 NICs**

	£
(£50,270 – £9,568) = £40,702 × 9%	3,663.18
(£53,000 – £50,270) = £2,730 × 2%	54.60
	3,717.78

Tutorial note

Self-employed taxpayers pay class 4 NICs based on their taxable trading profits. They pay 9% on profits above £9,568 up to £50,270, and 2% on any profits in excess of £50,270.

TASK 5

(a)   **Calculation of the gain**

	£
Proceeds	126,000
Selling expenses	(450)
Cost including acquisition expenses	(47,200)
Enhancement expenditure	(4,500)
Indexation allowance:	
on cost (£47,200 × 0.168)	(7,930)
on enhancement expenditure (£4,500 × 0.089)	(401)
Gain	65,519

Tutorial note

Costs incurred to facilitate the purchase or sale of an asset are deductible as allowable expenses in the calculation of a gain.

During the life of the asset, only costs incurred enhancing the asset are deductible, as these are capital in nature. Any costs of repairing the asset are not capital and therefore cannot be deducted in the calculation of the gain.

(b)

Any asset purchased by a company qualifies for rollover relief	
The amount of rollover relief claimed is deducted from the gain on the disposal of the new asset	
When making a claim for rollover relief, a company can choose the amount of gain to be rolled over	
For rollover relief to be available, the purchase of the new asset must be between 1 year before and 3 years after the disposal of the old asset	✓

Tutorial note

Rollover relief is only available for qualifying assets.

The amount of rollover relief claimed is deducted from the base cost of the new asset, not the gain on disposal of the new asset.

It is not possible for a company to choose the amount of gain to be rolled over.

TASK 6

(a)   **Share pool working**

Description	Number of shares	Cost £	Indexed cost £
15 July 2012 – purchase	1,500	14,500	14,500
7 May 2013 – bonus issue 1:6	250	0	0
Total	1,750	14,500	14,500
Indexed rise July 2012 to Dec 2017 (0.149 × £14,500)			2,161
Total	1,750	14,500	16,661
5 Nov 2021- disposal (350/1,750) × £14,500/£16,661	(350)	(2,900)	(3,332)
Balance c/f	1,400	11,600	13,329

Tutorial note

The matching rules for a company specify that disposals of shares are matched with:

1   purchases on the same day, and then

2   purchases in the previous nine days (FIFO basis), and then

3   shares held in the share pool.

There were no purchases on the same day as the disposal, but there was a purchase of 400 shares in the previous nine days (on 31 October 2021). It is these shares that are deemed to have been disposed of first, with the remaining 350 shares (750 – 400) taken from the pool.

Indexation allowance is not required before recording a bonus issue, but is required before recording the disposal.

Indexation is not available after 31 December 2017.

(b)   **Gain on disposal of shares**

	£
Proceeds (750 × £16.80)	12,600
Matched cost (400 × £15.50)	(6,200)
Indexed cost (from pool)	(3,332)
Gain	3,068

Tutorial note

The calculation of the gain could be split, as shown in the alternative working below. Either presentation would gain full marks in the assessment.

Alternative presentation of gain on disposal of shares

	£
Sale of 400 shares matched with purchase in previous nine days	
Sale proceeds (400 × £16.80)	6,720
Cost (400 × £15.50)	(6,200)
	————
Unindexed gain	520
Less: Indexation allowance (N/A)	0
	————
Chargeable gain	520
	————
Sale of 350 shares from the pool	
Sale proceeds (350 × £16.80)	5,880
Less: Cost (see pool working)	(2,900)
	————
Unindexed gain	2,980
Less: Indexation allowance (see pool working) (£3,332 − £2,900)	(432)
	————
Chargeable gain	2,548
	————
Total gain (£520 + £2,548)	3,068
	————

TASK 7

	First period **(12 months ended 30 September 2021)** £	**Second period** **(4 months ended 31 January 2022)** £
Trading profit	648,000	216,000
Investment income	12,240	4,080
Chargeable gains – 8 August 2021	319,000	
Qualifying charitable donations – 1 March 2021	(4,000)	
Taxable profits	975,240	220,080

Tutorial note

Companies with a long period of account must have their period of account split into:

1   the first 12 month of that long period

2   the remaining number of months in the period.

For the question above, this meant that we had to allocate the income and gains between a 12 month period and a 4 month period.

For trading income and investment income, this is done by time apportioning the total income, between the two periods.

For chargeable gains and qualifying charitable donations, this is done by allocation the whole gain or donation to the period in which it was incurred.

TASK 8

(a)   **Due dates**

    (i)   1 June 2022

           (i.e. nine months and one day after the end of the accounting period)

    (ii)   31 May 2022

           (i.e. 12 months after the end of the financial accounting period)

    (iii)   14 July 2022

           (i.e. 14th day of the 16th month after the start of the accounting period)

(b)   **Dominic**

	True	False
The maximum penalty for mistakes in a tax return due to carelessness is 50%		✓
A company with a period of account ending 30 September 2021 must pay a penalty of up to £3,000 if it does not retain its records until 30 September 2027	✓	
There are no circumstances in which client confidentiality can be breached		✓

(3 marks)

Tutorial note

The maximum penalty for incorrect returns depends on the behaviour of the taxpayer, and is calculated as a percentage of tax lost as follows:

(i)   Mistake despite taking reasonable care – no penalty

(ii)   Failure to take reasonable care – 30%

(iii)   Deliberate understatement – 70%

(iv)   Deliberate understatement with concealment – 100%.

A company must retain its records for six years after the end of the accounting period. The maximum penalty for not retaining records is up to £3,000.

The duty of confidentiality can be breached for legal or regulatory reasons (e.g. money laundering).